Lean in Agriculture
Create More Value with Less Work on the Farm

Lean in Agriculture
Create More Value with Less
Work on the Farm

By
Vibeke Fladkjær Nielsen and Susanne Pejstrup

A PRODUCTIVITY PRESS BOOK

First edition published in 2018

by Routledge/Productivity Press
711 Third Avenue New York, NY 10017, USA
2 Park Square, Milton Park, Abingdon, Oxon OX14 4RN, UK

© 2019 by Taylor & Francis Group, LLC
Routledge/Productivity Press is an imprint of Taylor & Francis Group, an Informa business

No claim to original U.S. Government works

Printed on acid-free paper

International Standard Book Number-13: 978-1-138-31770-3 (Hardback)
International Standard Book Number-13: 978-0-429-84742-4 (eBook)

This book contains information obtained from authentic and highly regarded sources. Reasonable efforts have been made to publish reliable data and information, but the author and publisher cannot assume responsibility for the validity of all materials or the consequences of their use. The authors and publishers have attempted to trace the copyright holders of all material reproduced in this publication and apologize to copyright holders if permission to publish in this form has not been obtained. If any copyright material has not been acknowledged please write and let us know so we may rectify in any future reprint.

Except as permitted under U.S. Copyright Law, no part of this book may be reprinted, reproduced, transmitted, or utilized in any form by any electronic, mechanical, or other means, now known or here-after invented, including photocopying, microfilming, and recording, or in any information storage or retrieval system, without written permission from the publishers.

For permission to photocopy or use material electronically from this work, please access www.copy-right.com (http://www.copyright.com/) or contact the Copyright Clearance Center, Inc. (CCC), 222 Rosewood Drive, Danvers, MA 01923, 978-750-8400. CCC is a not-for-profit organization that provides licenses and registration for a variety of users. For organizations that have been granted a photocopy license by the CCC, a separate system of payment has been arranged.

Trademark Notice: Product or corporate names may be trademarks or registered trademarks, and are used only for identification and explanation without intent to infringe.

Visit the Taylor & Francis Web site at
http://www.taylorandfrancis.com

Contents

Preface

We write this book because Lean is fantastic. We have seen the effect ourselves and cannot help talking about it. It is an excellent management concept for farmers who want to trim production.

What you can achieve with Lean is more satisfied employees and optimized processes. Both provide higher earnings.

Lean is based on certain principles, and to help you work with the principles, some tools are provided that are so simple and practical that they catch on immediately. They involve both employees and managers by having the daily work as their focus. Lean creates a structure for the good dialogue that everyone contributes to. Thus, everyone is committed to pursuing the goal.

Lean is not a project with a start date and an end date. It is a new way to think. Our ambition is that Lean will be a natural way of working. The new routines must be maintained, and the improvement work must be an integrated culture on the farm. Culture means that improvements and working positively with waste is an entirely natural mindset.

There is much money in Lean, we have discovered. So many things call to be picked up. Some of the improvements are in the pipeline for a longer time while others are seen straight away. That is how Lean has worked in a wide range of companies in other industries.

Now is the time for agriculture.

Vibeke Fladkjær Nielsen
Susanne Pejstrup

READING INSTRUCTIONS

Lean Management in Agriculture is written so that it can be read in different ways. You can read the book from end to end, you can skip between chapters and sections, or you can use it just as a reference book. Especially the section about tools is intended for referencing, depending on which tool you just need now.

Acknowledgments

Editorial Team:
Ann Møller Svendsen, Lean Akademiet ApS
Helge Kromann, SEGES, Danish Agriculture & Food council
Janni og Martin Fisker, farmers

Translation:
Mie Jakobsen

Drawings:
Claus Bekker Jensen, 2vejs kommunikation.

Special Thanks
To Ann Møller Svendsen for reading and academic sparring, and to Signe
Pejstrup for proofreading and cool remarks. Jens Kristian Jensen has been a great
help in testing our ideas, and Janni and Martin Fisker as well as Helge Kromann
have provided useful feedback on the book. Thanks also to Productivity Press
for cooperation on the book's release.

What is Lean?

Lean is about motivating and engaging employees in creating continuous improvement, in paying attention to waste in the production process and in creating more value for the customers and more earnings for the farm.

1.1 WHAT IS LEAN?

Lean means creating more value for customers with fewer resources. It is all about working smarter, not harder. It is about eliminating waste and using resources to work efficiently with the tasks. It is also about engaging employees in improvement, creating value for customers and thus value for the company.

1.1.1 THE LEAN HISTORY

The Lean history has everything needed to create a good story, as it tells the story of the leader who travels far and wide to find the philosopher's stone when his people are in need. He returns full of hope, and together with his people he finds the happy ending. It all started in the 20th century with the Japanese Toyoda family, who produced automatic looms. These looms were not like other looms. The fact is that they stopped automatically when the thread broke. None of the competing producers of looms had this feature. This meant that the employees in Toyoda's weaving mills could operate more looms at a time, and fewer manufacturing defects occurred. The patent on this fail-safe mechanism was sold in 1929, and the payment for the rights was used as initial capital in the Toyoda family's car factory, which was established at the beginning of the 1930s. In 1937, the factory became the Toyota Motor Company that we know today.

| 1900 | Craft production | 1930 | Mass production | 1960 | Toyota Production System | 1990 | Lean production in the United States and Europe | 2018 | Lean widespread in all industries |

In 1937, Eiji Toyoda went to the United States to study Ford's automobile industry. He noticed high productivity but also great waste, which got him thinking. He returned to Japan and started production. His son, Kiichiro Toyoda, was responsible for the company, which during the first years only produced trucks.

Kiichiro was an engineer and an expert in building engines, so he had a great understanding of production and manufacturing processes. Therefore, one of the basic ideas in Lean became that all leaders should know what is happening on Gemba (factory floor) because this is where value is created, and problems arise.

Toyota was well on its way to success, but then World War II came, and in 1950 Toyota was on the verge of bankruptcy. Like other countries, Japan got Marshall Plan aid to rebuild the country. As part of this reconstruction, a number of Japanese engineers were sent to the United States to study. They were taught production techniques by Professor Deming. His starting point was TQM (Total Quality Management), consisting of 14 points, which Deming considered the basis for efficient and flawless production. The Japanese followed his recommendations and put the theories into practice.

During a visit to the United States after the war, Eiji Toyoda had seen Ford produce 8000 cars in one day. Toyota produced 40. The Ford employees were ten times more productive than Toyota's. Nevertheless, Eiji Toyoda was disappointed that Ford's production had not changed since the 1930s. There was still too much capacity and excessive consumption of resources at Ford.

He also visited American supermarkets and was fascinated by the efficiency of retail supply chains in the United States.

This gave inspiration for a showdown with mass production. As it was, Toyota did not have the resources to mass produce cars, which would tie up capital unnecessarily in warehouse space. Taiichi Ohno asked Deming to come to Japan and help develop their production methods. This was the beginning of the production philosophy known as TPS, or "Toyota Production System".

After Eiji Toyoda's return, 1600 employees were asked to retire "voluntarily". This led to strikes and demonstrations. The management and employees at Toyota, therefore, entered an agreement: The employees were guaranteed lifetime employment in return for being loyal and actively working to create improvement in the company. This was the beginning of what we call Kaizen, which means "continuous improvement".

Eiji Toyoda asked his factory manager, Taiichi Ohno, to increase productivity to be up to the standard of Ford's. Ohno set two conditions:

- He wanted Eiji Toyoda's full support when resistance against the necessary changes arose.
- He wanted at his disposal every fifth employee released from production.

Eiji Toyoda accepted the conditions but with two reservations:

- No employees were to be fired. Therefore, as efficiency would increase, sales also had to rise.
- There was no money for neither new, big machinery nor warehouse space.

In addition, only the quantity demanded by the customer was produced and the customer always set the delivering time. Only what customers demanded was produced. This concept has since been called Just-In-Time (JIT).

Taiichi Ohno built on the principles and tools that Toyota had used until then. As he developed the techniques, productivity rose drastically. The methods were collected in the so-called TPS. The company achieved great growth, and productivity far exceeded that of other car manufacturers – also in Toyota's satellite factories in the United States.

CHARACTERISTICS OF A LEAN COMPANY

Focused: Lean organizations are obsessed with customer value.

Aligned: In a Lean organization, every member of the team understands the mission, values and strategic priorities.

Humble: One of the central tenants of Kaizen is that there is always room for improvement.

Collaborative: Silos have no place in the practice of Lean.

Tenacious: Lean organizations do not opt for simple answers to complex questions.

Engaged: Lean is a business process methodology that leverages the skills, input and observations of every employee.

Methodological: Improvement work is most effective when intentional practices are applied.

Proactive: Lean organizations inspect processes, not products, to prevent problems and waste before they happen.

Documented: Standard work is documented and continually reviewed.

Resilient: Resilience is the ability to anticipate trouble spots and improvise when the unexpected occurs.

Progressive: Realize that the improvement process requires the support of enabling technology.

Grateful: For Lean culture to take hold employees must feel valued and recognized for their contributions to improvement.

Revised from Maggie Millard, KaiNexus, 2015

1.1.2 LEAN – LESS OF EVERYTHING

During the 1980s and 1990s, more and more people discovered Toyota's success and started to copy their methods. Two scientists, Jim Womack and Dan Jones, went to Japan and researched for five years why Toyota was getting ahead of American car manufacturers. In 1984, they published the book *The Future of the Automobile*, in which they demonstrated that the Japanese car manufacturer outperformed American manufacturers on all key ratios. After this, they investigated what it really was that made the Japanese better than everyone else.

They found that Toyota had

- Fewer employees to develop, produce and service their products
- Less investment for a given amount of production capacity
- Fewer defects and less rework in internal processes
- Fewer suppliers, which in turn had greater expertise
- Less inventory at every step from order to delivery, and in after-sales service
- Fewer employee injuries and diseases

The code word throughout was less of everything, and the word Lean describes exactly that.

It was not until 1996, however, when Womack and Jones introduced the term "Lean Thinking" (in the book by the same name), that TPS won the West. Womack and Jones summarized TPS in some simple and easily understandable concepts, starting with the five Lean Principles:

1. Specify value from the point of view of the customer
2. Identify the value stream and eliminate waste
3. Ensure a steady flow of work
4. Replace push with pull
5. Continuous improvement

The five Lean Principles are the backbone of Lean and show you how to handle any Lean implementation. The principles are universal and can be used for production, administration and service. The principles are described in Chapter 3.

In Chapter 9, managers from other companies recount what they achieved by using the Lean Principles. It has not been without challenges, but on the other hand, they have had great returns. Thus, managers from Arla Foods talk about the company's growth strategy, where Lean is used as a method of generating capacity for growth without investing in new plants.

This is How Lean Can be Used in Agriculture

Lean is for all farms, small scale and large scale, that are open to change. For those open to change, Lean is the additional gear that provides increased earnings and greater employee satisfaction – without needing investment. Working with wastes has proved an eye-opener to the employees.

2.1 THIS IS HOW LEAN CAN BE USED IN AGRICULTURE

2.1.1 AN ADDITIONAL GEAR

Many farmers have standardized their procedures and continuously discuss "Best Practice" with their colleagues in an effort to improve. Farmers meet in groups to share experiences, and they are closely linked to companies and institutions that conduct trials and studies of production methods.

It has turned out that continuous improvement means that you are not satisfied with, for example, low mortality. Most skillful farmers can use Lean to get even better, Lean simply becomes additional gear. You also try to avoid animals dying, and instead make them grow well at a low feed consumption.

2.1.2 WHAT IS "VALUE FOR THE CUSTOMER" AT YOUR FARM?

In agriculture, the word *customer* means the consumer at the refrigerated counter. The customer can also be the company that buys the grain, or the slaughterhouse. However, in Lean terminology the word *customer* has another meaning, as the farmer himself can be both the supplier and the customer in a process or value stream.

Imagine the production of grain cut up into small steps. Each step in the process has a supplier at one end and a *customer* at the other. Thus, the next step in the process is the customer of

Only do what creates value

the part of production that you are looking at. The *internal customer* is thus the succeeding process in production.

CALVES MUST BE ALIVE – AND BIG

At a cattle farm, calf health had improved considerably through new procedures, change of feed and more systematic supervision. All calves born in the previous six months were alive. Owner and employees were proud of the result – and with good reason. They could not see what Lean could do for them in that respect.

Together, however, they made a value stream mapping (VSM). When they noted what was "value for the customer", it became clear that the weight also had significance. "The customer", which was in this case the heifer barn, wanted large, vigorous calves weighing 100 kg at eight weeks. It is a well-known fact that large calves do better and produce more milk in their first lactation.

At this farm, however, the calves were not weighed. The only thing that mattered here was if they survived. Therefore, Lean became the extra gear, which has now boosted the level of production. The calves are weighed, their growth is known, and 100 kg calves are delivered to the heifer barn.

Lean is about creating continuous improvement by eliminating waste. Waste is what *does not* create value for the customer. Therefore, in every stage of production, only make what creates value for the customer – that is, the next stage of the process.

2.1.3 AN EYE-OPENER FOR WASTE IN PRODUCTION

Waste is easy to spot when it lies as poor silage in the silo or germinated grain in the stubble field. It sounds boring, and you may think of situations where you have been annoyed by and tired of careless employees.

It is a common experience that when you start working systematically with Lean tools, it will be fun to find waste and come up with suggestions for improvement. It becomes a kind of treasure hunt – no lessons to give to employees.

You will clearly be bitten by it, because it is fun and motivating to help eliminate waste and bad workflows. We will tell you more about the waste types in Chapter 4.

2.1.4 MORE MONEY TO MAKE WITH LEAN

When you work with Lean on your farm, you will also introduce established standards, systems and routines. This saves time and provides a calm atmosphere when more people are involved in the farm. At the same time, it means fewer errors and more efficient workflows.

Since Lean tools involve employees in a positive way, they are not introduced with compulsion and control. Basically, you can also get your employees to earn more money for your business with Lean.

MORE PIGS THAN THE CUSTOMER ASKED FOR

In his farrowing unit, a pig producer had a skillful and ambitious production manager who wanted more piglets per year sow. He succeeded in rising from 34.5 piglets per year sow to no less than 37.8 piglets per year sow. The plan was to deliver the piglets at seven kg to the next step in production: the weaning unit. The number of piglets rose, but he did not manage to get them to seven kg, so they were delivered at an average of 6.4 kg.

But now the weaning unit had problems because the "supplier" delivered more piglets than the unit was designed for and even at a lower weight. This meant a worse result in the weaning unit because the daily gain fell, and the rate of disease increased.

The improvement opportunity lies in optimizing the overall cross-flow value stream, so that internal customers can also deliver what generates value for them.

2.1.5 LEAN PROVIDES MOTIVATION AND COMMITMENT

The Lean tools require involvement, and that will motivate and commit your employees. You will see new opportunities in them.

The board meeting is a good example. Of course, everyone at the farm is reluctant to commit himself or herself at the presentation of this working method. They think it's a little strange and unusual. Nevertheless, when the method is clear to everyone, things happen. The employees take over and start discussing how they can solve a problem. There are several suggestions, and they agree who does what. They become keen and committed. This is where involvement and ownership arise.

FORD ABOUT WASTE IN AGRICULTURE

In 1922, Henry Ford wrote in the book *My Life and Work* about waste:

The farmer makes too complex an affair out of his daily work. I believe that the average farmer puts to a really useful purpose only about 5 per cent of the energy that he spends. If anyone ever equipped a factory in the style, say, the average farm is fitted out, the place would be cluttered with men. The worst factory in Europe is hardly as bad as the average farm barn. Power is utilized to the least possible degree. Not only is everything done by hand, but seldom is a thought given to logical arrangement. A farmer doing his chores will walk up and down a rickety ladder a dozen times. He will carry water for years instead of putting in a few lengths of pipe. His whole idea, when there is extra work to do, is to hire extra men. He thinks of putting money into improvements as an expense. Farm products at their lowest prices are dearer than they ought to be. Farm profits at their highest are lower than they ought to be. It is waste motion – waste effort – that makes farm prices high and profits low.

Source: Ford, Henry; with Samuel Crowther: My Life and Work, *Garden City, New York, USA.*
Dear Henry Ford. It's a bit of a sweat! If from heaven you could see agriculture today, you would be surprised. Nevertheless, you still have a point!
(From Susanne Pejstrup's blog)

The Five Lean Principles

Lean is based on five basic principles that in their simplicity are called "The Five Lean Principles". The principles are key elements of the Lean mindset, so we will explain them individually and give examples from agriculture.

3.1 IDENTIFY VALUE

Only produce what has value for the customer. Value for the customer can be a somewhat unfamiliar concept when talking about internal customers. You may be both a supplier and a customer in the process – and to whom should you pay the most attention? The answer is, only consider your "customer side", that is, produce what has value for the customer.

When describing what creates value for the customer, be precise. If, for example, you have chosen to look at the part of production called "feed production", there is both a supplier and a customer: The supplier is the fields, and the customer is the cows. Then you must describe what will create value for the cows. What requirements do they have for the feed compound you produce? It is not enough to say that they should have "good feed". Be precise.

When you are precise, you know both what to do to meet the customer's requirements and what not to do. The latter is equally important when you deal with waste. If, for example, it does not add value to the customer to feed six times a day, you should not do it. And if it adds value to feed at fixed times, you should do it. It is all about doing what creates value for the customer, neither more nor less.

Milking cows

| Delivery: |
| 5 am-1 pm-9 pm |
| Quantity: |
| 30 kg DM / cow / day |
| Quality: No variation |
| follow receipt, fresh |

EXPERIMENT

Imagine that you call a company and order eight packages of 100 kg delivered every Thursday.

Would you accept that there are six or maybe ten packages? Moreover, they do not always come on Thursdays, but just as often on Fridays. Nor is there 100 kg in each package – the weight fluctuates between 60 kg and 90 kg and never reaches 100 kg. In addition, it often happens that one of the packages is broken on arrival.

Of course, you will not accept that. You call and complain. Perhaps you change supplier.

But what if you are the supplier? What if "calves" replaces the word "packages"? You need eight 8-week-old heifer calves of 100 kg every Thursday, if your production is to run optimally.

Then you cannot accept six or maybe ten ~~packages~~/calves. Moreover, they do not always come on Thursdays, but just as often on Fridays. Nor does each ~~package~~/calf weigh 100 kg, but the weight fluctuates between 60 kg and 90 kg and never reaches 100 kg. In addition, it often happens that one of the ~~packages~~/calves is ~~broken~~/ill.

This implies many opportunities for improvement:

- Leveling of calvings
- Better reproduction to avoid shortage of calves
- Fixed procedures so that moving the animals takes place on a fixed day of the week
- Weighing, more milk and control of daily growth to reach 100 kg
- Better procedures and housing, so that the calves are healthy at delivery

3.2 MAP THE VALUE STREAM

The second principle is to identify the value steam and eliminate waste. Only do what creates value for your customer – also your internal customer. And do it in the most efficient manner using as few resources as possible, that is, with the least possible waste.

The value stream is a new word. What does it really mean? When you work, you create value. For each process and each movement, you create value. You move feed from the silo, mix it and place it in front of the animals. That is a value-creating chain of actions – or a value stream.

FAILED TO SEE THE CONSUMPTION OF RESOURCES

An arable farmer had an analysis conducted on how to plan soil preparation before wheat seeding. The manager was very concerned with the quality of "the good seedbed", giving less thought to time consumption. The most important thing for him was to do the job properly. When a field was ready, he started work even though the tractor driver had to go far to get to the field in question. They often drove crisscross over the fields of the farm. They had the tradition of adhering to normal working hours in the daytime, so sometimes a tractor driver had to drive many miles back and forth in the tractor to get home for the evening.

Both the method and culture challenged the capacity, so often they were not ready to seed within the best period, and it meant additional costs because they had to hire in a contractor to do some of the work. They had never thought what harrow depth and tire pressure meant to fuel consumption. Actually, they did not measure fuel consumption. Nor did they measure other resources such as time consumption, in or outside the field.

To analyze the process, the employees put brown paper on a gate in the machine shed. First, they described how the good seedbed should be to satisfy the best establishment of the plants (customer requirements). Then the workflow was described systematically, with a yellow note for each step of the process. By going through the process again, it became very visible where they wasted time and other resources. They also realized where they needed data to make real improvement.

There was a very good atmosphere during the analysis, and many jokes came up throughout – plus many good suggestions for improvement. The quality would still be at the top!

3.3 CREATE FLOW

Flow means that work flows without unnecessary stops. Flow helps make work efficient. You will probably recognize it from many situations on the farm:

Flow in milking
Flow in harvest work
Flow in moving animals

Harvesting is a good example. When trailers arrive at an even pace, you can feel the value of flow.

The milking parlor is another place where flow is of great importance to efficiency. You can influence the flow by considering the following:

How many cows do you prepare at a time?
How many milkers are there in the milking parlors compared to the capacity?
In addition to milking, how many different tasks should be performed, for instance hoof flushing, treatment of diseases?
Do you have many slow-milking cows?

Different people ensure a steady flow of work with varying degrees of success. Therefore, Lean is a good way to form a general view.

FLOW IN SILAGE MAKING

At a dairy farm, making grass-silage is planned in detail to keep the same flow throughout the day.

They start with four trailers on the fields furthest away. The four trailers are the same size, and each can hold 40 cubic meters. The owner of the farm has requirements as to the size of the trailers and the interval in which they arrive. That will leave time enough to pack the grass properly before the next trailer arrives, and neither the trailers nor the loader tractor will have to wait.

If smaller trailers were used, they would not arrive at the same rate, and time would be wasted.

Later in the day, when the fields closer to the farm are chopped, only three trailers are used. And later again, when the fields close around the farm are chopped, only two trailers are needed.

Loads will arrive at the silo at the same rate throughout the day, leaving optimal workflow for the tractor loader. In addition, it is easy to pack the silage well. By continuously adjusting the number of trailers, the contractor expenses are optimized: The only thing you pay for is what provides an optimal flow and optimal packing.

3.4 ESTABLISH PULL

Pull means that you only produce what your customer wants and not what you have the capacity for. It also means that you do not start producing until your customer needs the product, that is you produce the amount the customer wants, and at the time the customer wants it.

This also applies to internal suppliers, for example your farrowing unit as the internal supplier to your weaner unit, which in turn is the internal supplier to your finishing unit.

Your fields are the internal supplier to your feed production, which in turn can be the internal supplier to your sows.

If you push all the young pigs that you produce through the system, you have 'push production'. You may not need all the young pigs, and it may not be profitable to make gilts out of them. The solution is to sell the surplus of young pigs and tune the farrowings so you only transfer the ones you need. Thus, you have a so-called pull production.

A good example from another line of business is McDonald's, which constantly has a production of two to four burgers of each kind ready for sale. Behind the shelf, an employee produces another burger every time a customer orders one. They might have chosen to produce 100 burgers on an assembly line to be ready for the big bustle at 5 p.m. That would, however, generate a great waste if only 80 were sold or if the customers suddenly wanted other kind of burgers.

The same system is used in tractor production. On one hand, when you order a new tractor, production only starts the moment you have placed your order. On the other hand, it is designed just as you want it, which produces less waste. In addition, you get exactly what you want to pay for – neither more nor less.

ASSETS DETERMINED HIS PRODUCTION

A farmer had a piece of land that was very suitable for production of Christmas trees. It would also save him some machine replacements, which would otherwise have been necessary if he had continued grain production.

He therefore planted the land up with Normann spruce, which was very popular among his colleagues. Throughout the next seven years, he tended the crop by weeding and fertilizing and adjusted the plants to be ready for sale. He had spent many resources, both costs and hours.

As he had no sales contacts himself, he sold the plants through a Christmas tree company. However, just the year when his trees were ready for sale, the market was saturated because, seven years earlier, several countries had planted a great number of trees. He was therefore forced to sell his trees at a much lower price than he had anticipated, and it turned out to be a bad piece of business.

The problem for the farmer arose because he let his assets, namely the piece of land and the machines, decide what to produce. It is called "push" production.

3.5 CONTINUOUS IMPROVEMENT

One of the central principles in Lean is continuous improvement. With the original Japanese expression, it is called Kaizen. Kai means change, and Zen means good.

The Lean principle is central because Lean cannot be implemented as a single change in production. There must be many small improvements. Therefore, we also talk about a Lean culture.

Employees must be involved, because those who work with things on a daily basis are the ones to come up with suggestions to improve. Improvement will never come about if only executives have fostered the idea.

Continuous improvement can be many things. In Lean, it is thought of as small improvements that can be implemented for next to no money. It might be making a gate for the hole, where the animals are always stuck. Or painting the tools in different colors to make it clear where they belong.

EMPLOYEES FOUND IMPROVEMENTS

In a vegetable production operation, the employees were annoyed because too many products were discarded by the buyer. They worked hard to do a good job and regretted that their product failed. That annoyance was their driving force.

The employees knew that the discarded products came from a field where the plants had had poor growing conditions. Thus, many of the vegetables did not have the proper shape and color. The easiest thing was to discard everything, but that was not possible. That way, one type of waste turns into other types of waste when you are not acting consistently. They therefore had to find alternative ways of improvement.

The solution became a Kaizen workshop in which customer requirements were defined for a start. Together, the employees then described the complete working process, and they reached a suggestion to improve that would reduce the amount of discarded plants.

1. In specific parts of the field, the vegetables were harvested by hand, and the bad ones remained in the field.
2. They introduced an additional screening before the vegetables were packed.
3. They found a customer for the vegetables that were OK apart from a wrong shape.

They agreed on many changes, and the employees were committed because they were the ones to find the solutions.

In the image below, the five Lean Principles are drawn in a wheel. The fact is that it is not a project that you can start on a particular date and end on another. It is a working method that you must use over and over again. You must create an improvement culture.

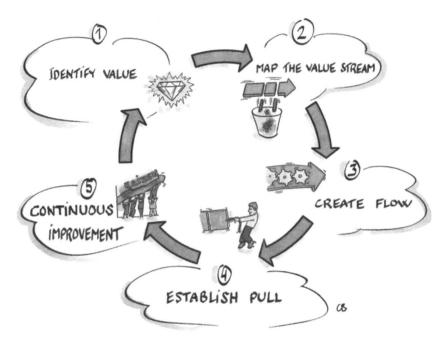

The Eight
Wastes of Lean

The core idea in Lean is to eliminate waste in production. Waste can be grouped into eight types, and once you have learned to see them in production/in everyday life, you cannot help suggesting improvements.

4.1 THE EIGHT WASTES OF LEAN

The core idea in Lean is to eliminate waste in production. Waste can be grouped into eight types, making it easier to recognize waste when you see it.

The Eight Wastes are:

1. Defect

2. Overproduction

3. Waiting

4. Non-utilization of talent

5. Transport

6. Inventory

7. Motion

8. Extra-processing

When everyone at the farm knows the eight wastes of Lean – and you talk about them – improvement suggestions will automatically appear. You simply can't help it. You can't say that a working procedure is awkward without thinking how to improve it.

4.1.1 LEARN TO SEE

- **First, you must learn to identify waste**. You can train it, read about it, talk about it and compete about it. Make a value stream mapping (VSM) of a workflow or process. It makes waste very visible when you map what you do – step by step. You can read about VSM in Chapter 7.
- **Write wastes on green sticky notes, one thing on each note**. Green is the color of hope, because when you have found waste there is hope of improvement. It is good to find waste, and it is good to find errors: It is the only way to create improvements. If you hide errors and explain away waste, you cannot improve. Be aware, if you begin to apologize and explain away. Of course, there are explanations, but you must still see it as waste.
- **You put the green sticky notes on the improvement board**. Then you can deal with them on your next board meeting. Here you can discuss the improvement suggestions, prioritize them and write them on the action plan.

4.1.2 EXAMPLES OF WASTE

4.1.2.1 DEFECT

1. Unclear workflows cause waste. If your employees do not know exactly what to do, they make mistakes and spend time asking and figuring out what to use.
2. If good colostrum is destroyed by strong heating in the microwave oven, the immunoglobulins that are so important to the calf are wasted. In fact, in that case it is a waste to use colostrum.
3. It is a waste of time to care for sick animals if you can avoid it by using another procedure.
4. Dead animals are a significant waste of work, feed and other resources.
5. If a pig only gains 500 grams a day and its potential is double that, we also talk about waste. Twice as many days are required to reach a weight of 100 kg.

6. We talk about waste when your employees do things in different ways, and the results therefore vary in quality.
7. If you have incorrect loading equipment and no instruction, damage may occur to the packaging.
8. Poor storage of feed and products means mold and discarding.

4.1.2.2 OVERPRODUCTION

1. If you produce more vegetables than the contract states, you risk getting a lower price or having to destroy the excess.
2. If your reproduction is good, you may produce more heifer calves than you need. If you still finish them as pregnant heifers without having a market for them, it is waste because the price will be too low.
3. We talk about waste if you produce more feed compounds than the animals eat.
4. It is also waste if you produce more grain than you can use or sell at the right price. Grain stored too long loses value and causes inventory costs.

4.1.2.3 WAITING

1. You wait for water filling a tub, milk getting warm, a reluctant animal to move, a machine driving somewhere else, an employee trying to find the adjustable spanner and so on and so forth.
2. Waiting time arises when you are waiting for a hauler to deliver a load, but he has not received the correct address.
3. An employee may wait ten minutes for water to run into the sprayer.
4. We talk about waste when an employee is thawing out water pipes with a blower for 15 minutes every morning.

15,000 NON-PRODUCTIVE DAYS – $22,500.

In a herd, calving age is 27.1 months. That is not unusual, but it is 3.1 months more than necessary. In addition, the dispersion of 2.8 months is far too wide.

This means that each heifer has 94 non-productive days. The herd produces 160 close-up heifers, which amounts to 15,000 non-productive days each year. There is a cost of at least $1.50 per day for feed, housing and wages. Waste totals $22,500.

4.1.2.4 NON-UTILIZATION OF TALENT

1. We talk about waste if you only see the hands and not the head of your employees.
2. It is also waste if not all employees are involved in making improvements – from production manager to the youngest apprentice, and all nationalities.
3. We also talk about waste if an employee participates in a course or discussion group with others, without trying out what he or she has learned.
4. We talk about waste if an employee does not have appropriate tasks, so that his/her talent – for example, animal care – is not utilized.
5. It is also waste if the manager does not involve employee creativity when a process is to be changed and improved.

4.1.2.5 TRANSPORT

1. We talk about waste if you use too large or too small machines or if you drive too far or too often.
2. External storage entails more transportation, and often you need to drive back and forth to pick up the loader.

3. If your animals are housed at several locations and you drive one way with an empty load, you have waste of transportation.
4. If logistics in your production plant are not good, every day you need to drive more than necessary.

4.1.2.6 INVENTORY

1. The whole secret is to have the right amount of feed. It can be expensive to have too little, but it is waste to have too much. The feed loses value, costs liquidity and requires additional storage.
2. It is waste to buy large quantities if it means discarding leftovers or if more storage is required. Many farms have old spare parts or building materials lying about.
3. We talk about waste if, for example, you have to buy fertilizer that is more expensive because you are short of storage or your stores are filled with many other things.

4.1.2.7 MOTION

1. When you put products and goods at a temporary spot, because there is no plan for the place, you will need time for an extra move. That is a waste of energy.
2. When you repeatedly need to look for tools that are not put back where they belong.
3. Many stacks give more stacks to cover every day. This can be avoided by ensiling in layers.
4. We talk about waste if the loader shovel is too big, causing you to drop things. Then you have to get off the loader to clean up.
5. It requires extra moves if you have to get on and off the tractor many times during a work process because gates, for example, must be opened manually.
6. It entails incorrect and extra movements if you have not placed things at the right height and distance when, for example, you pack your products.

4.1.2.8 EXTRA PROCESSING

1. We talk about waste when you clean just to clean, if, for example, an employee spends half an hour every day to clean the milk taxi on the outside.

2. An employee was convinced that the calf should have milk from its own mother the first three days after calving, instead of having quality-controlled milk from the colostrum bank.
3. We talk about waste if you clean the liquid feed plant too often, because that way you impede the biological processes in the liquid feed.
4. We talk about waste if, in the insemination unit, you inseminate the sows several times a day, instead of focusing on the optimal time and the correct stimulation of the sow.

Question:
It is not waste to have outdoor storage when it is cheaper than building a bunker silo?

Answer:
Outdoor storage can be the best solution in the short term. However, it still involves waste of transportation costs, time, feed and quality compared to other solutions. Maybe you can find other solutions than building a bunker silo.

Question:
When we work with waste, it easily turns into criticizing each other. How do we avoid that?

Answer:
You must pay close attention to using positive dialogue. Make sure that whenever you see waste, everybody knows that it is an opportunity to come up with improvement suggestions, making production better and work smarter. Never criticize what you do today. It must be a continuous process with the goal being constantly to improve. And only together do you improve.

Question:
How can it be waste to produce all the grain possible in all my fields?

Answer:
We talk about waste if you do not create value by doing it, because your costs become too large and the price of your products is too low. You should not produce just because you can but because you get a financial return.

Involve Your Employees

To create continuous improvement, it is necessary to involve your employees. You will not succeed if you push the improvements through orders from the top. This chapter discusses both Lean management and elements from other management theories.

5.1 INVOLVE YOUR EMPLOYEES

Involving your employees requires a different management style from the one we know best, namely the hierarchical.

COMPETENCIES DEPEND ON MANAGEMENT

"The employees who 'cannot figure out anything' at work can both be football coaches, build carports and repair cars in their spare time. It tells you something about management at the workplace".

Henrik Danielsen, Patriotisk Selskab

How do I motivate my employees, is one of the questions that managers often ask. It is not that easy, you see. You may think that the employees are the ones who must change.

There are actually many challenges with "uncommitted employees" who "do not show an interest" in the job. The solution, however, is not that the employees "must pull themselves together", but that the management style they are met with must be changed. People who are ordered to go from A to B cannot commit very much to that. If they do not get the opportunity to see the connection and influence the process, the job will not be inspiring.

INVOLVEMENT IS CRUCIAL

At a farm, which, among other things, produced groundnuts, the manager was really good at making schedules and visually showing how the standards were at the farm. One day he had made a new standard for driving the truck.

He put up great posters and was very pleased. But soon he realized that the employees did not comply with the new standard at all.

We discussed why they did not comply with it. He had a hard time realizing that employees do not take ownership until they are involved in discussing and setting up the standards.

5.1.1 TRADITIONAL, MODERN MANAGEMENT AND LEAN MANAGEMENT

With Lean management you look more across processes, you work in teams and you communicate in feedback loops with your immediate superior. In Lean, the employees need to be involved, and the best way for the manager to do that is to take a step back. This does not mean that the manager is invisible, but the management style is different.

Traditional management is often defined as management that is largely based on orders, rules and control. With traditional, modern management, we mean a management style that is controlled from the top but whose intention also is to commit and motivate the employees, work with values and so forth.

That management style is probably the most common in companies today – also in agriculture. The top management makes strategic plans and sets performance goals that employees are informed about and measured by.

Henrik Bak, who heads Arla's internal Lean office, Global Lean Management, says that Arla makes a dedicated effort to Lean train managers and middle managers. "For many years, managers have learned that a "true leader" leads the way, takes initiative, shows authority, makes decisions and so on. That is how a real leader appears, and that is also true of managers and middle managers in agriculture. Lean management, however, requires managers to step back – and that is hard for them", says Henrik Bak.

5.1.1.1 A DEVELOPING MANAGEMENT CONCEPT

Lean came into existence in the industrial society. It is created by the curiosity and involvement of the employees – focusing on increased productivity through continuous improvement. It required a management style different from the one used at the assembly line. But focus was on the operational aspect – on the processes. There were no tactical and strategical perspectives in the beginning.

Traditional, Modern Management	Lean Management
We look up to top management.	We focus on the customer.
Top-down management authority.	Management responsibility runs across the organization.
Middle management is measured by various target figures at the end of a period such as key performance indicators (KPIs) and budget follow-up.	Middle management is measured by process status with rapid feedback loops. "If the process is right, the result will be right".
Management is convinced that a properly implemented plan will produce the wanted results.	An understanding that all plans are experiments and that they can only be evaluated through a problem-solving method like the PDCA (Plan–Do–Check–Act).
Decisions are made far from where value is created. Decisions are made on the basis of analysis data.	Decisions are made where value is created, e.g. in the barn with the employees. "Go and see, ask why, show respect".
Consultants, often only with a short-term contact with the middle manager, make standardization of procedures, and they are rarely revised.	The middle manager, in cooperation with the employee team, makes standardization of procedures, and they are revised often.

Since then, Lean has been further developed into more refined use, involving several other management methods. Thanks to that, Lean is used today in manufacturing, service, public administration and other industries. We can use Lean, although we have now passed from industrial society to knowledge society with a big focus on strategy.

LEAN – DESIRE, CREATIVITY AND EXPERIMENTS

The main driving force in Lean is not productivity, efficiency, profit, quality, prosperity and so on; it is people's intrinsic desire to explore the world and challenge themselves and others. Lean can never be achieved through goals, management, duty and so on, but can only mobilized through trust, conversation, knowledge, desire, inspiration and space for creativity and experimentation and so forth.

Preben Melander
CBS - Copenhagen Business School

Today, it is discussed whether it is possible to handle future demands with Lean. Some skeptics mention that the eternal pursuit of waste has resulted in too small a buffer – too little "fat". It may also be risky if some devices are only produced one place in the world. Then production becomes very vulnerable.

THREE THINGS LEAN LEADERS DO

- Make each employee identify waste, solve problems and improve his/her job.
- Ensure that each employee's job creates value for the customer and the company.
- Ensure time and space for continuous improvements.

Other skeptics mention that a management concept that is so focused on efficient production cannot handle a market driven by emotions and desire for experiences. Agriculture must also be aware of that risk. We think rationally and are focused on doing things in the best and professionally most correct way. We risk underestimating a customer demand based on emotions – which we may not understand and do not really recognize.

Therefore, it is not enough that the company is controlled by process optimization. It is necessary for the company to develop – also strategically. Lean is therefore not a complete recipe, but a concept with associated tools that will still develop.

5.1.2 MOTIVATION REQUIRES TRUST AND RESPECT

In his book *The 7 Habits of Highly Effective People*, Stephen R. Covey describes a breakthrough he had with his seven-year-old son. He wanted to teach the boy to take ownership of a task. The task was to be in charge of the lawn and make sure it was tidy. For a long time, he tried with different methods. He carefully showed his son how to do it and trained him to tell the difference between the right way and the wrong way, and he was close to tempting him with money and scolding him as nothing really helped.

The breakthrough came when he started listening and recognized that his son found the task difficult. When the boy understood that his father trusted him, something happened. The son asked, learned and took responsibility for the task. The lawn was tidied, watered and mowed all through the summer.

Another important aspect of creating motivation is respect for other people.

Respect is close to recognition; they are two sides of the same coin. If you do not respect another person, you cannot motivate him/her.

Try to think of situations from your own life, where you have been highly motivated by another person. It was probably a person that you appreciated and who respected you. Otherwise, you would have noticed it, and then you would not have liked to do anything for that person.

Very quickly, we notice whether we are met with respect. We read the body language, eyes, facial expressions and tone of voice of people close to us – especially if these people mean something to us. We can feel whether a person finds us OK or the opposite.

If you are with someone who does not respect you or think you are OK, it feels uncomfortable.

FOUR QUESTIONS ABOUT YOUR MANAGEMENT STYLE

Reflection for you who want Lean:
- How do you usually react when your employees tell you about problems in production?
- Which tools do you use for problem solving?
- Which model do you use to follow up on the changes you have made?
- Which system do you use to distribute employee time between development and daily tasks?

MOTIVATION WENT TO ZERO

A man was employed at a farm. There was a lot of focus on doing a good job and keeping everything tidy. He was keen on coming out of it well and constantly scanned the owner's body language to check if he did things right or wrong.

"One day", he said, "I had finished my work before the others had finished theirs, and actually, I could just have left. Instead, I went to the others and was just about to take a broom to help them finish. It would give me the opportunity to show initiative and a sense of solidarity with my colleagues, I thought.

I did not make it before the owner shouted: 'Grab a broom and help us finish!' Boo! I did it of course, but it was with a completely different feeling. He did not trust me, and my motivation went completely to zero".

That is a fact that is underestimated by many managers and employers.

Respect goes both ways. Your employees must also respect you if you are to succeed in motivating them to perform their best. And this applies to both professional and human respect.

That means that you must be fair and professional.

YOUR BODY LANGUAGE GIVES YOU AWAY

A farmer found it difficult to get his employees to take initiative by themselves. To him they seemed idle as soon as he turned his back. Therefore, he considered introducing PBR (payment by result) or a bonus system to create motivation.

He was basically of the opinion that foreign employees only came to make money and were not interested in doing a good job. "They do not care at all", he said, clearly annoyed and angry. "I have to stand over them all the time, otherwise they don't do anything properly".

He was asked how the employees reacted to his opinion of them. "I don't tell them, of course", he answered. He clearly was not aware that his body language gave him away long before he opened his mouth. You cannot motivate people whom you think are lazy and indifferent.

If there are things that you are incapable of, you must acknowledge it, don't just pretend.

1. **Show the Employees Respect – And Get Theirs.** People follow great leaders because they want to – not because they are told to do so. There are many ways to get people to follow you, but a good way to start is to show them respect. On top of that, you must be skilled and professional.
2. **Set High Goals for the Team.** It is much more fun and motivating to strive to obtain the highest yield than to go from average to +5%.
3. **Make Tasks Meaningful.** Tell your employees why you do things the way you do, so that everybody understands it. Provide them with the professional background for doing so. Commit the employees by including their proposals and ideas.
4. **Go For Increased Commitment.** People usually do what is expected of them. But they choose for themselves whether they will go to great lengths and do the exceptional. You must make them. Show that you trust them, and give them ownership of their tasks.
5. **Use a Visible Scoreboard.** Visible performance goals are motivating if employees can influence them. Choose some targets that can be affected daily. Make sure that there is a culture of continuous improvement.
6. **Make a Good Team Fabulous.** If your team thinks they are doing OK, you risk not developing anymore. You must constantly challenge, ask questions and benchmark to reach new heights.
7. **Talk About the Efforts of Your Employees.** Do not take the efforts of your employees for granted. Talk about them, and mention their achievements as often as you can.
8. **Avoid Being Negative.** Even though you do not always choose the challenges you meet, you always choose how to react to them. If you are negative, your people will be negative, and then you get nowhere.
9. **Immediately React to Poor Performance.** If you catch an employee performing below level, you must react immediately to reach the level you want. You cannot do that the day after, and certainly not at a joint meeting later.
10. **Make Time and Space for Coaching.** Teach yourself to coach to develop your employees in regard to knowledge, skills, attitudes and performance. Use coaching as a tool in your daily life as a leader.

MAKE GOALS SPECIFIC – AND OBTAINABLE

Goals must be broken down into sub-goals to motivate. For instance, it does not help on the football ground if the scoreboard says: We are heading for Champion's League! The scoreboard must show specific numbers, that is whether we are behind or in front – and by how much.

RESPECT – SOMETHING YOU ARE WORTHY OF

An employee had great commitment. He never left the barn until everything was in its place, and he made it a point of honor that production was running optimally. He was very good at taking care of the animals.

After a change of manager, it began to go downhill. The owner was well aware that they did not get on well, but he thought it would work out. The new manager complained about the employee, and with good reason. He had begun to leave a lot of mess, he left the barn, even if an animal needed help, and he was to be neither led nor driven.

At the performance interview, it turned out that the employee had no professional respect for the new manager. He was to decide, but he did not have sufficient professional authority – without realizing it himself, though. The manager himself was convinced that his education made him the most skillful. Unfortunately, the employee left the farm before the problem was solved.

BE POSITIVE – IT WORKS

All situations can be looked at from a negative and a positive point of view. You choose yourself how you want to react. If, for instance, an employee drives into a gate, you may choose to take it out on him and put your foot down: "Now, will you pull yourself together". However, he did not do it to bother you.

You may also choose to ask him what he did differently all the times he succeeded in missing the gate. Maybe he used another gear, maybe the lights were on or he wore other shoes, which did not slip on the pedal. The answer reveals what it takes to be successful. Thus, you teach him to focus on where he succeeds instead of where he fails.

5.1.3 APPRECIATIVE LEADERSHIP

Everybody needs appreciation. Appreciative words and actions help shape our identity and self-understanding. When we are appreciated, we have trust in ourselves and in others. We feel successful, and as a consequence, we are encouraged to think new ideas and perform even better.

To most farmers, it is crucial to be appreciated for their skills. It gives both joy and energy when things succeed and people notice it. This is true both when you receive a prize at the animal show, when colleagues from the discussion group speak highly of you and when an employee returns because your farm is a good place to work.

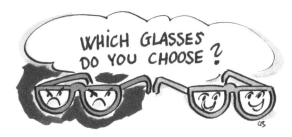

Appreciative leadership is a management style that can foster development of both people and companies.

WE WANT TO BE POSITIVE

I don't think that anybody gets up in the morning, leaves their wife/husband/sweetheart, parks their children in the care of other people and goes to work thinking that they want to be in opposition. I simply don't believe that. We want to be appreciated for what we do, we want a decent life, we want to be treated with dignity, we want to speak with each other, we want to be heard, we want to have an interesting and exciting job.

Henrik Danielsen

5.1.3.1 PRINCIPLES OF APPRECIATIVE LEADERSHIP

The principles of appreciative leadership are

1. Everyone has successes, and in these successes, there is scope for development.
2. Focus on what works.

3. People are different, and everyone has talents and qualifications, which should be brought into play.
4. It is clear to the employees what the good performance is and when the goal is reached.
5. Ongoing dialogue about the small victories puts focus on employee efforts.
6. You speak up to your employees and believe that people grow with responsibility and free hands.

5.1.3.2 SHARE GOOD EXPERIENCES

At the board meetings, one of the items on the agenda should be: "Share a good story from last week". All employees must contribute something positive from last week. In the beginning, they may hang back a little, as we are not used to praising ourselves. Therefore, it is OK to mention something impersonal such as, The sun was shining. That is a beginning.

Gradually, it is enjoyable to be at the board, as everyone has had their turn:

- "You were quick to respond as the sow was getting squeezed. Well done!"
- "We finished on time. Good work!"
- "I came here last night and everything was neat and tidy".
- "We have no sick animals this week".
- "We have now finished at 5 p.m. four days in a row".

It is a great point at a meeting that offers many benefits. The atmosphere is lifted, and everyone gets more energy. There is room for small and well-placed praise heard by everybody. At the same time, it provides you as a leader with the opportunity to show and articulate your values. When you say that everything was neat and tidy when you came to the barn in the evening, you show that it is one of your values.

> A board meeting is a brief, standing meeting at a board where the employees discuss suggestions for improvement.

You can read more about board meetings in Chapter 7.

5.1.4 CHANGE MANAGEMENT

It is hard enough to change yourself. But when you want other people to

> When we are filled up with praise, we are readier to change.

do something different, it will be even harder. It requires change management and knowledge about human reactions in change processes.

5.1.4.1 CULLBERG'S FOUR PHASES

Swedish psychiatrist Johan Cullberg conducted interviews with 59 people who had been through a crisis. He found that they underwent four phases when they worked themselves through the crisis. Moreover, he found that the same reactions could actually be seen in people who are subjected to change.

The four phases are

1. **The Shock Phase:** The phase can last from just a moment to several days. You simply don't understand what is happening. You try to deny it, you may be apathetic, and you reject it.

   Your employees will meet your improvement suggestions with great resistance in this phase. They might think you are joking. Or they may not respond at all.

2. **The Reactions Phase:** In the reaction phase, you start to understand what has happened. You react, you grumble. You get angry and sad, you feel insecure and afraid. You resist and argue.

   Your employees might take it out on their spouse or their colleagues. As a leader, you will see different reactions. They back out and declare that it will never work out. They will certainly be no part of it.

   You will also be unsure in this phase. Is it such a good idea? You ask yourself the question: "Should we rather leave it when they react so violently?" Then it may be a great help to know that there is a third phase.

3. **The Healing and Processing Phase:** In this phase, you begin to face facts and relate to the present. You are a bit up and down in this period.

   Employees who have been presented with changes begin, in this phase, to relate to them. They begin to find their place under the new conditions. They begin to speak constructively about what is going to happen. With coaching, you can help your employees to see their new roles and how they can influence the new procedures.

4. The Reorientation Phase: The final phase is the reor  in which you begin to make plans for the future. You have coped with the difficulties and get back to work again.

In this phase, your employees will suggest how to implement the new initiatives. They will have "bought" the idea and support it.

RESISTANCE FROM MANAGER SLOWLY OVERCOME

The four phases can also be recognized in minor change processes. At a farm, we were to introduce board meetings. It was a decision the owner had made without really informing anybody. Obviously, that was a blunder that made everything more difficult.

During the opening speech, the manager was silent. His body language revealed that he thought it was far-fetched. His attitude was contemptuous and indulgent. He was in phase one.

When they came into the barn, he was clearly in the reaction phase. He was in opposition, answered sullenly and, most of the time, he was standing behind the others with his arms crossed. He made a call on his cell phone and went back and forth. Several times, he said that the proposed suggestions were impossible. He was clearly in phase two. Unfortunately, it also affected the two workers who had been positive to begin with.

The owner, however, succeeded in imposing the board meetings. The manager was still somewhat negative, but not quite so demonstrative. It was agreed to take turns being in charge of the board meetings – one month at a time. The manager also headed meetings, and gradually he started to participate in the process. There was a minor crisis at a time when he repeatedly accused the owner of not completing the agreed actions on time. The manager was now in phase three.

After a few months, it started to work. The manager had developed his own model for the board meetings together with the workers, and they found the meetings useful. He had finally reached phase four.

5.1.4.2 CHECKLIST FOR CHANGE MANAGEMENT

John P. Kotter, Harvard Business School, has set up eight steps to go through to succeed with change management.

1. **Create a Sense of Urgency:** You must describe an opportunity that will appeal to your employees' heads and hearts. Use the statements to raise a large urgent army of volunteers.
2. **Build a Guiding Coalition:** This means that there must be consensus on the change between owner and manager. If there is no consensus and support, it will fall to the ground when the least resistance occurs.
3. **Form a Strategic Vision and Initiatives:** Create a vision and a strategy to realize the vision. The better people can envision where they are going, the more they can focus on specific initiatives that make the vision a reality.
4. **Enlist a Volunteer Army:** Tell the story on every possible occasion to make many employees join. It is important that owner and managers lead the way in spreading the positive message.
5. **Enable Action by Removing Barriers:** Change systems and structures that counteract the changes. Encourage your employees to come up with ideas and to take initiatives.

6. **Generate Short-term Wins:** It is important to create visible and rapid results and to praise employees who contribute to effecting improvements in the process.
7. **Sustain Acceleration:** Every day you must adapt and change systems, structures and guidelines incompatible with the vision. You must balance between change management and change leadership.
8. **Institute Change:** Explain the connection between the new behavior and the success of the company. You must develop tools that can ensure that the change is maintained.

There are some good recommendations in Kotter's eight steps to good change management, and the recommendations are well in line with the Lean mindset.

5.1.5 COMMUNICATION AND QUESTIONING TECHNIQUE

5.1.5.1 COMMUNICATION TYPES – WE ARE DIFFERENT

In working with Lean a good use of questions is important, especially in three situations:

1. To commit people during board meetings.
2. When, together, you have to find the core of a problem – that is, a problem-solving method.
3. When you work with value stream mapping.

We humans express ourselves in different ways, depending on how we see the world. This may give rise to many frustrations, so it is good to know these differences. When you know that some people take a long time answering, it is easier to accept.

LONG RESPONSE TIME

A farmer's wife said about her husband, who was the introvert type, "When I ask him something on Mondays, I sometimes get a response on Wednesdays".

Types of Attitude

The Extrovert Type   We all know the extrovert type who loudly plunges into all discussions. They are often spontaneous and quickly begin to speak. They can easily dominate at a board meeting because saying something is easy to them. They are not always as good at listening to others and are quickly bored when others speak. They are valuable at a place of work because they make fun and get things

going. To them dialogue is important, because it is often only when things are put into words that they realize what they think about a matter. This type is best at developing ideas when speaking with others, and they may have difficulty reflecting on their own.

The Introvert Type   In a group of employees, some are also more introverted. They are more reserved, and therefore they risk being misunderstood. As they do not immediately express themselves, others may think that they are less gifted or stupid.

It is by no means the case, but they need to chew a bit on the matter, to think before they speak. When you as a leader ask the group direct questions, the introvert types often will not respond. You may be annoyed and say it is impossible to draw a word from

them. However, that will worsen the situation, as the introvert type needs confidence to play an active part. If they are confident and with people they know, they can easily express themselves, and their contributions are often good and carefully prepared.

Types of Lifestyle

The Assessing Type   To people of the assessing type it is important to take a position, to classify, to put things in place in a logical system. They want to settle questions and plan activities. Their way to communicate may seem harsh to others, because they are so direct in their communication.

The Observing Type   To the observing type, senses and intuition are important. They take things as they come and do not assess whether what other people say is good or bad, true or false. They just note what the other person thinks. In a discussion, they take in new information and may change their mind, which other people may perceive as indecisiveness.

People are different and express themselves differently. It is important that you consider that when you are to be the leader of a group of employees. The two types of approach and the two types of lifestyle can be combined, enabling us to recognize four ways to express ourselves.

5.1.6 USE OF QUESTIONS IN LEAN WORK

Extrovert assessing type	Introvert assessing type
Extrovert observing type	Introvert observing type

5.1.6.1 TRAINING

It is important that everybody contributes, even if they don't say anything right away. Therefore, the leader must be aware of including everyone. That requires practice and training. Not everyone can do it just like that. Training can be attending a course in speaking techniques or inviting a coach to the farm.

There may be a tendency to have a dialogue between the leader and only one participant. But the dialogue should include everybody. The participants are a team.

5.1.6.2 THE IMPORTANT CONFIDENCE

It is also important that everybody feels confident. Leave out hidden agendas such as using board meetings to "make employees say it themselves" if they do something that the owner doesn't approve of.

Also, raise your voice if some of your employees are laughing or ridiculing a colleague who speaks out.

That is poison for the process. You must stop that immediately by initiating a joint agreement on rules or maybe even a "friendly talk".

5.1.6.3 OPEN QUESTIONS AND PAUSES

You may turn directly to someone with a question, but also be aware that some people are actually getting performance anxiety and find it very unpleasant if they are confronted.

Open questions and pauses are good tools for this purpose. When using interrogatives, be aware that in some contexts they can be perceived as criticism. If you ask a colleague: "Why did you do it?", he or she may perceive it as criticism even though it was not intended that way. You may rephrase the question to "What was the reason that you chose to do it that way?"

If, at the board meetings, you are very specific and talk about daily routines, it is easier to include everyone.

Examples of questions starting with what, when, who, which, how and why:

- What do you see as the reason?
- When does it happen?
- Who do you think knows how?
- Which solutions to the problem do you see?
- How do you see that it affects the workflow?
- Why do you think the animals react as they do?
- Which solutions do you propose?
- When will we get there?
- What can I do to help?
- What would happen if we chose to do that?

> Open Questions Start With
> - What
> - When
> - Who
> - Which
> - How
> - Why

5.1.7 TALKING STICK

The use of a Talking Stick can make the employees listen to what is being said and keep the discussion focused. The method can also provide the quiet person with the courage to speak, because he or she knows that nobody else will speak as long as he or she holds the Talking Stick.

Talking Stick originates from the Native Americans where it was used to solve conflicts between contending parties and to achieve a conversation respectful of all arguments. Today, the method is used in several contexts and in a more developed form than mentioned here. But this simple way works very well when you are standing in the barn.

Only the person holding the Talking Stick is allowed to speak. Everybody else must listen and try to understand what is being said. When he or she has finished speaking, the Talking Stick is put forward. The next person who wants to speak will then take the stick.

A Talking Stick is not necessarily a stick or piece of wood. You may choose whatever you like, for instance the pen that you already hold in your hand.

5.1.8 CATCHBALL

Catchball is a method that ensures consistency between what you are looking for as a leader and the ideas that your employees have. It is an effective way to get the whole farm to work together. Such a process may take a couple of weeks.

At catchball, you must agree that ideas are thrown back and forth between the top leader, the farm manager and the other employees.

You may achieve the following with catchball:

- The team is involved in making the plan and thus gains ownership.
- You ensure management commitment to ideas from the team.
- Everyone who has inputs to present do so.

FROM INDIVIDUALISTS TO TEAM

Catchball helps involve people more as members of a team than as individuals.

Charles Tennant

THROWING IDEAS LEAD TO SOLUTION

At a vegetable farm, they had problems retrieving transportation boxes from the storage room. Two persons were always needed for the job. The manager said, "We have a challenge, retrieving the transportation boxes. What do we do to enable one person to do the job?"

The employees discussed it. They realized that the location of the storage room was the challenge. Based on that recognition, the ideas were now thrown back and forth.

- One employee suggested that they built a new flat storage to avoid storing the boxes up high. Then one person could retrieve them.
- Another was of the opinion that they exchanged the pallet lift for another type. That might solve the problem.
- A third suggested that they rearranged the storage facilities, storing items that were not used very often up high instead.

The suggestions were turned over and over. Then the question, How much can a solution cost? was returned to the leader. The answer was that they had to find a good solution below $2000.

This excluded the suggestion of a new building, and the employees proceeded with the other suggestions.

That way the problems were thrown back and forth until a solution was found in which the employees were prime movers.

5.1.9 COMMUNICATION WITH STICKY NOTES

Sticky notes are a good tool when more employees participate in the decision-making process. They are good because they provide visibility. You switch from oral to written communication while being compelled to express yourself briefly. They can be moved, so you can physically move a proposal from one priority to another and so on. Here are a few examples of how you can use sticky notes.

5.1.9.1 THE BOARD MEETING

Sticky notes are the obvious choice for board meetings. During the week, you can put up suggestions for improvement. The person in charge of the board meeting can hold a suggestion in his/her hand as you discuss it. Then you can put it somewhere else on the board, for instance in the priority section. Everyone can join, and spelling and language are subordinate. You may also draw suggestions.

5.1.9.2 BRAINSTORMING AND PRIORITIZING

If you want your employees to come up with a lot of ideas and afterward agree on which ones to choose, the following method is good:

1. You are silent and reflect individually for ten minutes. You write all your ideas on sticky notes – one idea on each note.
2. Initially, put all sticky notes in a fishbone chart enabling you to get an overview of whether the idea belongs to "management", "manpower", "method" or "machine".
3. Then you can take a group of ideas, for example under "management", and prioritize them in terms of effect and effort. You can read about the prioritization method under board meetings.
4. The next step is to decide which ideas you want to implement.
5. The final step is to put them into an action plan or project plan for the ideas that are more complicated to implement.

There may be more good ideas than you can implement right away. You can put them on a to-do list or set a date later.

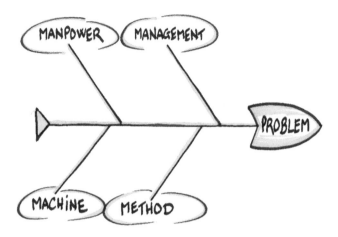

APPRECIATE YOUR PROBLEMS

Problems are like treasures – valuable to discover and fun to solve. You'll even get praise when you find them!!!

Pascal Dennis, Getting The Right Things Done

5.1.10 FIVE WHYS

Five whys is a technique to get to the core of a problem. We tend to extinguish the same fire over and over again because we do not find the root cause. We are too quick to address the immediate cause without getting to the core.

In 1988, Taiicho Ohno from the Toyota factories described a simple method called Five Whys, that is, 5 x why. "By asking 'why' five times and answering the question each time, you'll get to the root cause of the problem, which is often hidden behind the first symptoms", Taiicho Ohno explained.

Taiicho Ohno gave the following example with a machine that had come to a standstill:

1. **Why did the machine stop?**
   There was an overload, and the ignition went out.
2. **Why was there an overload?**
   The bearing was not sufficiently greased.

3. **Why wasn't it greased?**
   The lubrications pump did not pump properly.
4. **Why didn't it pump properly?**
   The shaft was worn and rattled.
5. **Why was the shaft worn?**
   There was no tightening, so a metal piece had come in.

FIVE WHYS IN THE MILKING PARLOR

The morning milkers start at 4 a.m. and discover that again, there are no clean wipers. That is annoying, and therefore at the next board meeting, they suggest to buy some more. However, they start with the five whys:

1. Why are there no clean wipers?
   Nobody has started the washing machine.
2. Why hasn't the washing machine been started?
   Because it can't run when the washing program for the milking parlor is on.
3. Why can't it run when the washing program is on?
   Because the relay turns off.
4. Why does the relay turn off?
   Because the electrical system becomes overloaded.
5. Why is the electrical system overloaded?
   Because there is a defect in the way it is set up.

Lean literature mentions that problems should be solved slowly. That is to say that every time, you have to make sure that it is the right problem you solve. We are used to making quick decisions, but then you risk solving the wrong problem.

Question:
I see the idea with sticky notes, but I think that my employees will turn it down because they think it is too freaky.

Answer:
It is a different way to communicate. It is easier to break daily patterns if you introduce it as a new method – maybe helped by an advisor. Call a meeting and introduce it as a new initiative – make a story out of it. It is our impression that most people quickly understand the idea, and that it works well.

Question:
How do I get my employees to go for my goals for the company?

Answer:
You are the one to decide the overall goals for your company. You must involve your employees in breaking the goal into subsidiary goals and then into daily actions. When, at the board meetings, you talk about performance management, they are committed to reaching the daily goals. The goals you measure must be connected to the overall goals.

Question:
How do I get the quiet employee to talk?

Answer:
Some people need time for reflection. You must respect that. Take your time to listen. You must ensure a good and confident atmosphere, and you may agree with your employee that he/she contributes with something specific at the next meeting.

Question:
How can I show respect to an employee that I don't respect?

Answer:
You can't. Nevertheless, you must respect him/her, and maybe you need to revise your view of human nature. Everyone has potential, and you must learn to see it. You must acknowledge the starting point of each individual. You must also listen to him or her – that is, really listen with the intention to understand. When you acknowledge and understand your employee, you will be able to motivate, train and build from there. If you still don't respect him/her, he/she is probably the wrong employee for you.

Question:
How do I get my employees to take initiatives? They are just waiting for me to speak.

Answer:
Step back, and have confidence that they can do it. Many have seen their employees perform incredibly well, while they themselves were on holiday. If you are fast and enterprising, they will not challenge you in that position. They will await your signals.

Question:
How do I get an employee to take responsibility?

Answer:
The simple answer is involvement. When people are informed and involved, they also take responsibility. You can't take responsibility if you don't understand the background of what you are doing. Here is an example from a farm where two apprentices joined the vet at an animal welfare inspection tour, while the foreign trainees did not. The foreigners were subsequently criticized for not observing the animals sufficiently.

Question:
In Lean, you look for waste, and in appreciative leadership you look for the positive. Is that not a contradiction?

Answer:
No, there is no contradiction. It is positive if your employees can identify waste. It shows that they see where value is created. In addition, at the same time, they are appreciated because they know and come up with improvement suggestions.

When you identify waste, it is possible to eliminate it and hence improve your earnings. If your employees are not able to identify waste and tell you about it, you don't have the opportunity to eliminate it. However, you should also pay attention to focusing on the improvement opportunities.

Question:
I find it difficult to hand over responsibility. What if it goes wrong?

Answer:
It can be very difficult. You must hand over responsibility gradually to be certain that your employees can handle it. That way your confidence in them will increase. Often, they can do more than you think, so sometimes you must keep cool. Finally, you must be ready to accept solutions other than those you would choose.

Question:
My employees will not change old habits. What do I do?

Answer:
Try to read about the four phases we are all going through when we are introduced to something new (Cullberg's four phases). Some people are in the reaction phase for a very long time. Habits can only be changed if you are willing to do it yourself. Therefore, you must involve your employee, enabling him/her to suggest how change can happen.

Question:
What is the difference between ISO and SOP?

Answer:
ISO (the International Organization for Standardization) is a quality management system, ensuring that everybody in a company does as agreed. It is supervised by an external company. SOPs are standard operating procedures which, quite true, have the same purpose but with less control. In agriculture, we make SOPs for smaller areas and for certain simple work procedures when we find it necessary. It may be a single page with pictures that the milkers make to visualize a joint decision.

Question:
The manager puts a stop to it all. She is very negative and can ruin every-thing. What do I do as the owner?

Answer:
First, find out if there is a power struggle behind it. Perhaps she is unsure, and maybe she is the type of person who is not good at changes at all. It may also be that she just needs more time. Remember, the Lean work might be something you pull down over her head. Lean management requires that the middle manager employs a new management style, and that leads to uncertainty. We suggest that you give her more knowl-edge and training in Lean management, leading her to safer ground.

That is How You Work with Goals

6

Continuous improvement and change management require a goal. A good goal motivates and provides energy, and involvement provides committed employees. By breaking down goals and having clear goal management, you achieve results.

6.1 THAT IS HOW YOU WORK WITH GOALS

6.1.1 THE BURNING PLATFORM

When you want to create change in your company – for example, achieving a goal you have set – you must be prepared to do things differently, and you must include your employees.

It is natural human behavior to be reluctant to do something different because it always entails a risk. We prefer to stay in familiar settings where we know our way round – our so-called comfort zone. It is always uncomfortable to move in unfamiliar surroundings. Unless we are on a burning platform. If we see that action and change is necessary to survive, we move.

It is therefore necessary that you visualize the burning platform to make change occur. There must be a ticking bomb under the table or a sense of "this can't go on much longer".

It is certainly discussed whether we humans only move away from something or if we move toward something too. Can change be created by drawing a future image toward which people want to move? Probably, to a certain extent. But it is undoubtedly necessary with a burning platform to get people out of their comfort zone.

Examples of burning platforms:

- The bank has demanded operating credits reduced before the end of the year.
- Earnings must be raised 20% to ensure survival.
- Someone should be fired if earnings do not increase.

6.2 WHAT IS A GOOD GOAL?

A good goal is motivating and provides energy. When you describe the goal accurately, in the present tense and the first person, it seems present, personal and motivating.

6.2.1 INVOLVE YOUR EMPLOYEES

There are several advantages to involving your employees in setting goals:

- Employees are more likely to work in a certain direction,
- once they have been involved in setting the goal.
- It becomes a more qualified goal when more people are involved in setting it.
- It is easier to accept a goal that may differ from your own wish once you have participated in the process and know the reasons.

> Hoshin Kanri is the name of one of the Lean tools. It is a method of breaking down the overall strategy for employee goals and actions.

SMART Goals Have Five Criteria to be Met

	EXPLANATION	EXAMPLE
Specific	What should I do? What must be met? The goal is precisely formulated and delimited so there is no doubt what you mean.	The cost of maintaining machines must be reduced.
Measurable	How do I see that the goal is met? It must be measurable, preferably with numbers.	The costs must be 10% lower in six months.
Accepted	The goal should be accepted by the employees, and they should be able to influence it.	The employees should participate in breaking down the goals and make action plans themselves.
Realistic	It must be obtainable, on one hand, so we do not lose motivation. On the other hand, it must also be ambitious, so there is something to go for.	Benchmarking shows us that it will be possible.
Time-based	When is the goal fulfilled? Possibly write milestones. You must know when in goal.	We must follow the costs every week and reduce by 0.4% per week for the next 26 weeks.

6.3 BREAKING DOWN OF GOALS

Breaking down of goals into day-to-day goals is difficult. In agriculture, key ratios are used, which on average go back 12 months. As an example, herd yield is expressed in liters/cow/year. Crop yields are measured in tonnes/hectare. We are so used to these figures that we also see them as goals for our employees: "Our goal is to rise to 12,000 liters of milk/cow/year!"

However, it does not seem immediately motivating to employees because they cannot directly influence the figures. Moreover, they cannot see the connection between the goal and the daily effort. They realize that they should do well, but what exactly does that mean? This is why you should break down the goal, and like the tennis player Caroline Wosniacki says, "I only look at the next match and the next ball".

AN EXAMPLE OF BREAKING DOWN OF GOALS

- Better production economy
  - Number of disease attacks should be reduced
    - Better monitoring and earlier treatment

6.3.1 PERFORMANCE GOALS AND EFFORT GOALS

There is a difference between performance goals and effort goals. An example of a performance goal is, I will win the championship in ten km cross-country running next year. An effort goal could be, I will run ten km every second day. The performance goal indicates what you want to achieve. The effort goal describes the effort needed to achieve the performance goal.

6.3.1.1 PERFORMANCE GOAL

What you choose to go for makes a difference. If you only go by performance goals, you can release energy and creativity in your employees because they have freedom of method. They themselves find ways to reach the goal. Very quickly, they can change a procedure if they see that it is a good idea. Moreover, they can learn lessons along the way.

THEY ACHIEVED THE GOAL

A farmer had set a goal to improve the economic profit per hectare by 5% while expanding by taking over one more farm. It was an ambitious goal, as he knew that results usually drop at an expansion. Still, he believed that there was a potential, which he wanted to make use of.

He set up an action group consisting of his managers, tractor drivers, an advisor and himself as a team leader. The group was called together, and he presented the goal. They were then asked to break down the goal, that is find out which day-to-day goals were needed to reach the 5% increase.

FIRST BREAKDOWN

The group found three important areas. One of them was to ensure that man-hours and machine hours were utilized more optimally. It was discussed what the goal should be and how they could measure it. They chose to make time registration and combine it with the timetables of the machines, so they included the hourly consumption both in the field and outside the field. They made a forecast, which they subsequently reduced by 5%.

SECOND BREAKDOWN

So as not to end with a weak statement of intent, it was necessary to have the overall goal translated into very specific daily goals that all employees could act on. It should also be made into their responsibility – not just something the owner should look at.

They therefore set up a list of eight things that they influenced, and which would affect hourly consumption per hectare: Preparation, Maintenance, Transport Time, Breakdowns, Share of Reduced Tillage, Tilling Depth, Implement Width and Cleaning.

They decided to measure in all eight areas with a continuous focus on how to manage more hectares in less time. They also decided to have a short meeting over the phone every morning to discuss the results on the board. Every day they wanted to learn from the experiences from the day before.

They achieved the goal of an increase of 5%.

We will produce cheaper in two years

Now: Costs are 90% of revenue   Goal: Costs are 75% of revenue

Labor cost per unit must be reduced before the end of the year

Nykælverne skal fra nu af minimum følge niveau for 10.500 kg på laktationsnøgletallene ved 2. kontrollering.

Now: 0.52/unit   Goal: 0.45/unit

In three months, our time consumption per week is lower

Now: 372 hours/week   Goal: 350 hours/week
                                                 point

The figure shows an example of how to break down goals into something that is easy to relate to as an employee and easy to measure.

Effort goals are easy to measure and to make visible, enabling everyone to see if the goals are achieved. That way it is easier to get all employees to do what is needed. Not much technology is necessary to measure effort goals. In many cases, it is just a matter of counting marks and drawing strokes.

Effort goals may indicate that what you measure turns out well, but you may not achieve the results you expected. It can therefore be "dangerous" to measure only on effort goals.

BETTER REPRODUCTION	HIGHER PRODUCTIVITY
Performance goal:	Performance goal:
Calving age of 24 months next year	10% more units per working hour in a year
Effort goal:	Effort goal:
Weighing of all heifers every month	Three improvement suggestions at every board meeting

MORE TIDINESS	LOWER COSTS
Performance goal:	Performance goal:
All stores of rubbish gone before new year	10% less repackaging of cucumbers
Effort goal:	Effort goal:
One 5S process every month	Adjusting the packing machine every hour

6.4 GOAL MANAGEMENT

When you use goal management,

- You move in the same direction
- You know what is important
- You know if you are approaching the goal
- You have the opportunity to adjust if something goes wrong

"A pig doesn't grow fatter by being weighed", they say, but measurements provide an overview, and actions provide improvements. Therefore, goal management must be attached to action. Goal management and Kaizen/board meetings are connected.

The main purpose of goal management is to provide and visualize information, which can be used when eliminating waste. At the same time, goal management is a way to communicate and visualize where you are now and where you want to go. The goal management board is the main tool.

You look at the goals you want to work with. Then you examine the situation now and in a possible future. Finally, you define the contributions needed to achieve the goal. You set a deadline and agree on who is responsible.

Always remember that measurements are only information. If you don't share the information, it is worthless. Conversely, measurements in a usable form are extremely effective – yes, they may be the glue that holds the entire project with value stream management together.

> ### SERIOUSLY AND FOR FUN
>
> Can you imagine a basketball game without a scoreboard? No, because it is so central to both energy and strategy that you can follow the position. We don't need it when we play for fun in the backyard, but then both level and performance are something entirely different.

6.4.1 VISIBLE GOAL MANAGEMENT

When you visualize goals and results, your employees will be more motivated to participate in creating improvements.

People learn in different ways. Some are visual and prefer to use their eyes to learn. Others are audial and learn best by listening. A third group is characterized as tactile. They learn best by using their hands. A fourth group – the kinesthetic – learn best by using the body.

Not everybody finds a print with a lot of figures interesting. You should use that knowledge to motivate your employees to reach your goals. You should use several different tools, for example graphs, colors, pictures, dialogue and actually going to the relevant location in production. That way it is easier to motivate all your employees, regardless of their preferred way to learn. At the same time, communication with foreign employees is improved.

> ### USE MORE TOOLS
>
> Use different tools, for example graphs, colors, pictures and dialogue. Or go into the production and look at things.

Graphs are an effective tool. They are easy to understand. They communicate with more than figures and words. It is easy to see whether something is rising or falling. Moreover, graphs create an emotional reaction: When the curve goes the wrong way, the employees want to do something about it. When an improved result is shown as a rising curve, they feel rewarded. No one needs to say it; the results are visible to everyone. It provides a sense of pride that,  every day, you pass a board with a curve that you have helped turn upward.

6.4.1.1 CONTRIBUTION TO REPRODUCTION – VISUALIZATION WITH MAGNETS

Example:

In the insemination and gestation unit, they wanted visual goal management of the returners. The team had decided to focus on the young female pigs the next month. They would turn a negative trend.

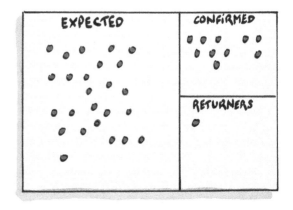

They made a board with a magnet for each of the 36 young female pigs they were going to inseminate, of which they expected 33 to be in-pig.

They moved a magnet whenever a young female was confirmed in-pig. They agreed to have only three magnets in the "returner" section. Visualization gave focus.

6.4.1.2 CONTRIBUTION TO IMPROVED SAFETY

Weeks without accidents

Goal: Max. five per year

Week 1	Week 2	Week 3	Week 4
Week 5	Week 6	Week 7	Week 8
Week 9	Week 10	Week 11	Week 12
Week 13	Week 14	Week 15	Week 16
Week 17	Week 18	Week 19	Week 20
Week 21	Week 22	Week 23	Week 24
Week 25	Week 26	Week 27	Week 28
Week 29	Week 30	Week 31	Week 32
Week 33	Week 34	Week 35	Week 36
Week 37	Week 38	Week 39	Week 40
Week 41	Week 42	Week 43	Week 44
Week 45	Week 46	Week 47	Week 48
Week 49	Week 50	Week 51	Week 52

Safety was not good enough on the farm. The manager and the employees had specified a goal of reducing accidents leading to illness and treatment to five cases a year.. At the same time, they had decided on the contributions to reach the goal.

They then agreed that each week without an accident was a success. They started in week 33 and celebrated the successes, thus motivating everybody to do their utmost to avoid accidents.

It also gave rise to a professional discussion about how accidents happened. A culture of improved safety was forged.

6.4.1.3 MAINTENANCE OF MACHINES – RECAP OF TOTAL NUMBER PER WEEK

WEEKLY MONTHLY		ACHIEVED	STATUS
17	73	15	−2
17	73	17	−2
17	73	20	+1
17	73		

At a vegetable farm, they had systematized maintenance of machines.

However, they often found that maintenance was given a lower priority when urgent repairs were needed. Therefore, they made this chart, which by a simple count made it possible to continuously monitor development in relation to the goal on a weekly and monthly level. The manager had calculated how many machines needed to be maintained each week to reach the goal of number of maintained machines. Every week, they counted and made status. It was visible and clear to everyone whether they were able to reach the goal or needed more manpower.

6.4.1.4 COWS IN HOOF-TRIMMING BOXES – RECAP OF TOTAL NUMBER

WEEKLY MONTHLY		ACHIEVED	STATUS
20	80	15	– 5
20	80	25	0
20	80		
20	80		

Getting the cows through the hoof-trimming box is a task that is easily left out in busy periods. You can always trim some more tomorrow! And the day after, you say the same thing.

This chart enables you to manage the contribution goal of hoof-trimming 20 cows every week. You make counts, and everybody can see how you are doing compared to the goal.

When hoof health improves, you may decide to reduce the number.

6.4.1.5 TIME CONSUMPTION

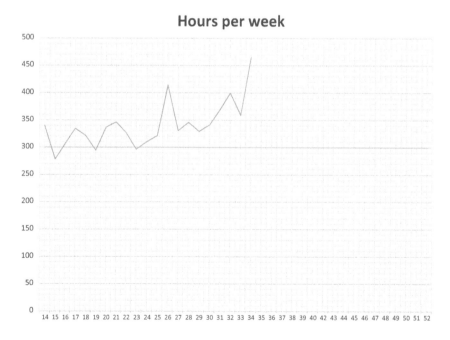

Hours per week

Graphs are good because they are visual. It is better to show the weekly time consumption in a clear graph than in a column of numbers in the office.

This graph is made in Excel and only requires you to enter the number. Then, the graph is generated automatically.

It also works if you use a pen. The purpose is to visualize the measurements you use to reach your goal.

6.4.1.6 VISUALIZE WITH A GREEN AND RED COLOR

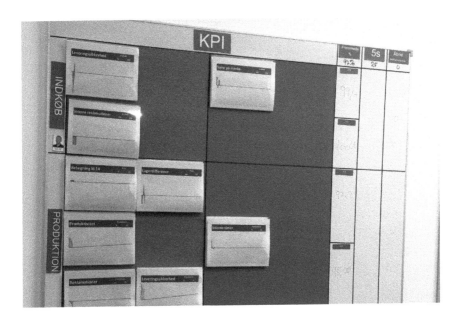

You can also visualize by making a green and a red section on the board. You can then place your KPI measurements with magnetic pockets depending on whether they are above or below the target. KPI stands for key performance indicator.

6.4.1.7 LIVE-BORN CALVES – VISUALIZATION

Example:
At a farm, they had the goal more live-born calves. The employees were taught what caused stillbirths, and they made an action plan.

One day when the farmer was in the mall, he saw an offer of plastic balls to play in. He immediately bought a lot of them, after which he went home and found a huge glass vase.

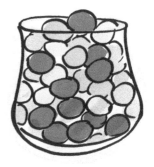

It was decided to put a plastic ball into the vase every time they had a live-born calf. And for each ball the owner would pay $5 to a bowling evening for the entire employee group.

6.4.1.8 VISUALIZATION OF PRODUCTION

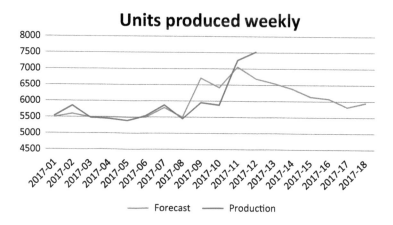

This curve shows what can be called "Stay on track". KPIs show whether production is running as planned. This information is important for employee motivation and commitment

6.4.1.9 TRAFFIC LIGHTS

With measurements, you can achieve continuous improvements and standardization.

Goals		Results
Higher than 95	◖	88
Below 200.000	◖	180,000
8 per week	◖	6
12 per week	◖	14
More than 10	◖	9

Excel is a great tool for making your goal management online. With the "Conditional Formatting" feature, you can get automatic "traffic lights", so there is a color marking of which goals you have achieved and which you have not reached.

6.4.2 ACTION PLANS

When you have set a goal and broken it into milestones on a daily level, you must agree on the actions needed to reach the goal. You must do something different to make change. Examples could be

- Employees must be involved in deciding what to do. They must make the suggestions. If you are short of professional knowledge, then invite an expert. But you must choose the actions yourselves.
- Action plans must follow the SMART principle, that is, be Specific, Measurable, Accepted, Realistic and Time-based. Do not make do with "We'll do it as good as we can". It must be SMART.
- Make one person responsible. It may take more employees to carry out the plan, but appoint one employee to take the initiative and to follow up. When choosing the responsible person, do not make the same person responsible for everything. You both risk leaving the person with too little time, and you fail to commit everybody. It gives commitment to be responsible of something – be it big or small.
- Follow-up must be agreed and written down – both who, when and how. You may use the PDCA circle to visualize where in the process you are. PDCA means Plan–Do–Check–Act. Put the circle on the action plan, and hatch a section to indicate where in the process you are.

> Many Names For the Same Thing
> Action plan, list of actions, contribution plan are all the same thing.

6.4.3 EXAMPLES OF CONTENT IN ACTION PLANS

6.4.3.1 MAINTENANCE OF MACHINES MUST BE SYSTEMATIZED

- We will make a new general standard operating procedure (SOP) on maintenance this month. Responsible: Peter
- We will make a new whiteboard with an annual survey of all machines to be put in the workshop. Responsible: Paul
- We will make two workshop trolleys containing everything needed for regular maintenance to have everything close at hand. Responsible: Peter
- Everybody must be instructed in proper lubrication of all machines. Paul makes a plan for the instructions.
- Better lubrication pumps. Peter checks up on them every Thursday.
- Lubrication oil: A new product may need to be tested. Paul looks into it in the coming week.

6.4.3.2 DIARRHEA IN CALVES MUST BE STOPPED

- The temperature of the milk must be measured. Peter buys a thermometer and makes SOP next week.
- Calf bowls must be cleaned every day. Paul takes a picture of clean calf bowls and puts it up tomorrow.
- Feed troughs must be cleaned every day. Peter puts it on the work plan today.
- The calves must be fed colostrum very quickly. Paul checks prices on various colostrum systems before next meeting.
- Make a chart for registering when every single calf was born, when it was fed colostrum, the quality of colostrum an so on. Peter makes it tonight.

6.4.4 VISIBLE ACTION PLANS

The action plans must also be visible. Below, we show different methods.

Goal: No lame cows in the barn and max. two in the hospital pen.

6.4.4.2 WHO DOES WHAT AND WHEN?

NO.	WHAT ?	WHEN	WHO ?	PDCA
7.	Take 5 cows into the Hoof-trim box monday - Toesday - Wednesday	Start week 3	Peter	◐
8.	Make a place on the weekplanner to write bad hoof on	Today	Paul	◑
9.	Go for a walk in the barn Find examples of bad hoofs	Thusday week 4	Sarah	⊕
10.	Make a training course for everyone on the farm.	Monday week 6	Peter	⊕
11.	Make a fohoof-bath for the heifers every Tuesday	Start week 4	Joan	⊕
				⊕

6.4.4.3 ACTION PLAN FOR LESS BREAKDOWNS IN HARVEST SEASON

Goal: To lower the breakdowns from 17 per week to below five per week.

Use the program SmartDraw to make MindMaps. It can also be made with sticky notes and handwriting.

The technical part is simple. You just make a pattern of text, drawings and pictures instead of writing in traditional dots. With a pattern, you will find it faster and easier to get an overview.

In this example, a drawing shows the six things it is agreed to do something about to achieve the goal of less breakdowns.

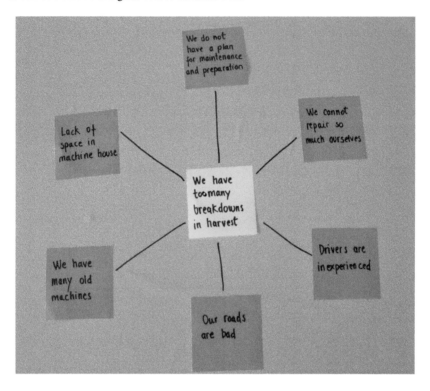

6.4.4.4 ACTION PLAN FOR HIGHER YIELD IN WHEAT

Goal: Next year the yield must be 9500 kg per ha on average.

No.	Activity	Responsible	Jan	Feb	Mar	Apr	May	Jun	Jul	Aug	Sep	Okt	Nov	Des	Status	Follow up
	Change species															
a1	Meeting with advisor	Peter														John
a2	Order seed	Paul														John
a3																
	More accurate seeding and better seedbed															
b1	Meeting with contracter	Peter														Tim
b2	Make activity plan	Paul														Tim
b3	Visit from advisor	Peter														John
	Better weed control															
c1	Advisor visit 1 - walk the fields	Paul														John
c2	Advisor visit 2 - walk the fields	Paul														John
c3	Evaluation	Peter														Tim

Tools

Lean methods are based on a number of tools. This chapter describes nine tools that can be used immediately in farming. The chapter can be used as a reference text to read about the individual tools.

7.1 TOOLS

This chapter introduces some of the Lean tools it is best to start with when a Lean vision is to be implemented.

You can use the chapter as a reference book and read about each individual tool. The following tools are introduced:

- WeekPlanner
- Kaizen meeting
- PDCA
- Value stream mapping
- Standardization
- 5S
- Kanban
- TPM
- SMED

The features of each tool are described under the heading You Can Achieve. Here, you can read how you can benefit from using the tool. In the section How To Do you can read how you actually use the tool.

Finally, we have gathered some of the issues we have encountered most often when farmers work with the Lean tools.

Enjoy the toolbox.

7.1.1 WEEKPLANNER

The WeekPlanner is used to plan the coming week. The planner is for quick and weekly adjustments of your regular work planning. It supplements the regular work plan.

The WeekPlanner is visible to everyone, and everybody can change and add. This works fast and is more flexible than if only one person is to make the changes on a PC.

7.1.1.1 YOU CAN ACHIEVE

- **Information.** All employees are involved and informed.
- **Overview.** It is clear which employee is responsible for a task if, compared to the regular work planning, it has been moved, for example because of illness.
- **Communication.** You get the opportunity to discuss special things happening this week.

- **Information across.** Teams can inform each other (e.g., we start construction on Tuesday).
- **Time saving.** It saves time, everybody knows the weekly plan.
- **Initiative.** Employees become more self-employed.
- **Structure.** Employees experience structure and systematics.
- **Tools for weekly meetings.** A good starting point for the weekly meeting with employees.

7.1.1.2 HOW TO DO

1. The WeekPlanner is a whiteboard, which should be placed at a prominent place in production. It should be located where you all pass by daily. The planner may be placed next to the Kaizen board and the board you use for printouts, changes to the regular work plan, messages and so on. You can think of the area as your "communication center". Your employees should always be able to find information here.
2. Write the names of your employees on one side and the days of the week on the other. You may also make a section for the coming week and one for the regular work plan.
3. You write the tasks that are extraordinary, which must be coordinated between the employees on the board. You can also inform each other about illness or birthdays. Examples of information: School children visiting, vacation and days off, participation in external meetings and so on.
4. You can print photos and names of employees on magnetic paper. Magnetic paper can be purchased in office stores and online stores. To most people pictures are quicker to understand, and they are absolutely necessary for people with a reading disability and foreigners who don't read English. A board with pictures is also more fun.

Question:
Where do I buy the boards for the WeekPlanner?

Answer:
You can Google "whiteboard" and find a retailer that way.

But make sure the boards have a ceramic surface and can withstand being in the production buildings.

Question:
Can't you be negative at the meetings at all, not even if something really annoys?

Answer:
No. Meetings are reserved for the positive dialogue. You must create confidence to make your employees participate with an open and trustful mind. It is not professional to let yourself be controlled by annoyance. If you want to tell someone off it must be at another time.

Question:
We surely cannot be discussing whether an employee can have a day off?

Answer:
No, it must be settled with the manager before the meeting. The WeekPlanner must be used to inform the others so that they know who is on duty and whether it affects their own tasks.

7.1.2 BOARD MEETING AT THE IMPROVEMENT BOARD – KAIZEN

Board meetings are brief meetings at an improvement board in the barn, workshop or production. The improvement board is a whiteboard placed centrally, close to production. It is natural to combine the board meeting with the talk about next week, now that you are together.

At the board meeting, you discuss how far you are, compared to your goals, and you can talk about new improvement suggestions.

7.1.2.1 YOU CAN ACHIEVE

- **Positive dialogue.** You talk constructively about work.
- **Involvement of employees.** They must contribute, and they are asked.
- **Visible goals and results.** Everyone knows what you are striving for.
- **Improvement culture.** You learn how to work in order to improve continuously.
- **Visible management.** Daily management is carried out both orally and in writing.
- **Team spirit.** You gather at the board and make improvements together.
- **Improved employee satisfaction.** Involvement entails satisfaction.
- **Improved earnings.** Tasks are solved in a better and better way.

With board meetings, you ensure that your employees are motivated for and involved in spotting waste and producing improvement suggestions. Employees are challenged to take responsibility for their daily work. In addition, the board meetings contribute to visualizing goal management, so everyone goes for the same goals and knows how actions affect the outcome.

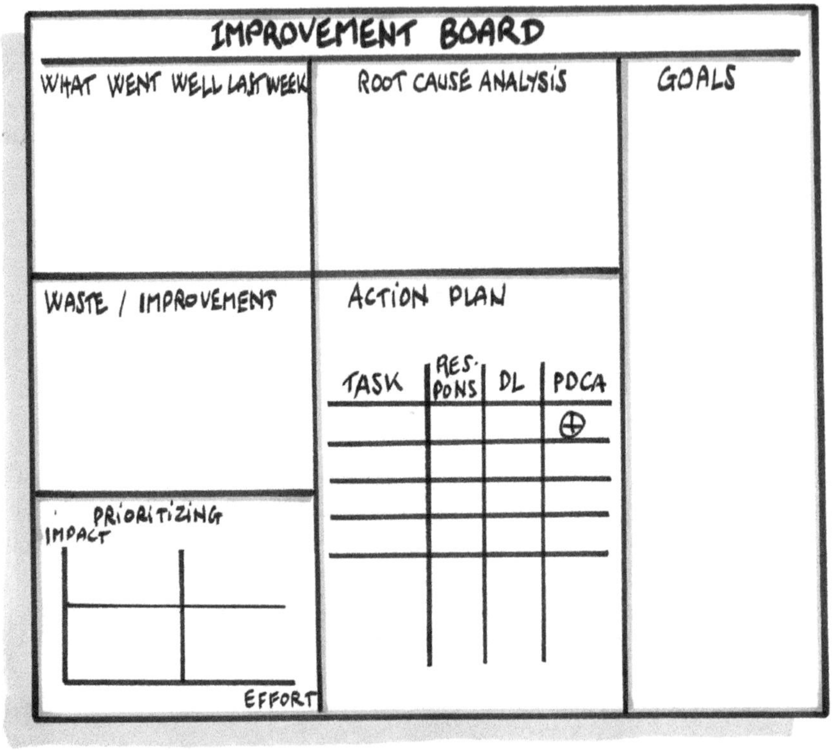

IMPROVEMENT BOARD

WHAT WENT WELL LAST WEEK | ROOT CAUSE ANALYSIS | GOALS

WASTE / IMPROVEMENT | ACTION PLAN

TASK | RES. PONS | DL | PDCA

PRIORITIZING
IMPACT
EFFORT

You create team spirit, and your employees are involved in decision making. That is a good step toward motivated and committed employees.

People's participation in a dialogue is affected by whether they stand up in front of a board where everything is visible to everyone, or if they are sitting at a table and each is writing on a piece of paper. There are more dynamics in a standing meeting, the minutes are made on the spot, decisions are made here and now and everyone can follow.

You can see the model in use in a detective story on TV, when a team is to find who the killer is. Here they also use a board as a dynamic tool in standing meetings.

7.1.2.2 HOW TO DO

- A large whiteboard is placed centrally. If you are short of wall space, you can use a board on wheels.
- The board is divided into sections with magnetic tape or a pen. The headings of the sections can be
  - Agenda
  - What went well last week?
  - Waste/Improvement

- Prioritizing
- Root cause analysis
- Action plan
- Goal management

The division must match the agenda you choose for the meetings.

- Length of meetings must be exact and agreed. They should only last between 15 and 20 minutes.
- Agree on a set time every week for the meetings. Choose a time when everybody can participate
- Agree on a set agenda.
- Agree how you will take turns being in charge of the board meetings.

ALARM AFTER 15 MINUTES

At a farm, they sat the alarm on the telephone to sound after 15 minutes, forcing the participants to end the meeting. "It was annoying at first, but now we have been trained in making it brief. And two employees no longer take up time discussing a nut", says the farmer, adding that the self-chosen time limit has given better energy to the meetings.

7.1.2.3 IMPORTANT ON AGENDAS

All meetings must have the same agenda. That way everyone knows what is going to happen. Each meeting is so short that there is no time to adjust to new items on the agenda. If you need to change the agenda, report it at the meeting the week before.

An example of items on the agenda:

Planning Next Week   The item only covers the special things that will happen next week. In addition, it is important that you only plan and inform about things that concern everyone. The others are wasting their time if Peter and Paul are using the meeting to discuss who is to participate in the meeting in the slaughterhouse.

What Went Well Last Week?   Each employee MUST mention at least one thing. It may be a personal praise to the others or to themselves. It provides a lot of energy to focus on what works and what you do well. As a leader, you have a great opportunity to praise your employees and, at the same time, exercise value management by commending initiative, order and cleanliness or whatever you want to promote. Your employees have the opportunity to acknowledge colleagues: "It was nice that you had folded all the boiler suits", or "It was nice that you handed over such a clean milking parlor to us at the morning team".

Goal Management   You have made a goal, which you have broken down into subsidiary goals. Under this item, you look at the progress in achieving the day-to-day goals. Likewise, you may decide whether to change your plans. Preferably, bring visible income statements that have been updated before the meeting. You may talk about a deviation to learn from it: "The machines were stuck ... Why? What can we do differently next time that situation occurs?"

Waste and Improvement Suggestions   On the board, there may be a section with the heading "Waste and improvement". If employees over the course of the week identify waste in production, they can write a green sticky note and put it on the board in this section. There may also be green notes from earlier on – notes that you have not had time to deal with yet.

Anyone can of course make suggestions at the meeting. Each proposal must be written on a pink sticky note and placed in the section on the board.

Prioritizing   Waste and improvements must be prioritized. The person in charge of the meeting takes one sticky note at a time, and you agree on prioritizing every single waste/improvement in relation to effort and effect. You may use a matrix, placing the suggestion in the appropriate square. The person in charge must remember to get acceptance from everybody, thus preventing making his/her own priority crucial.

1. Quick Wins: These are waste and improvements with a high effect and which can be obtained with a low effort. Therefore, you can address them immediately.
2. Fill Ins: The waste/improvements don't require a high effort, and they don't have a high effect, either. They must be initiated but do not have a high priority.
3. Plan as Project: Waste/improvements have a high effect, but also require a high effort. They may require more planning and involve more employees. They may be initiated now but will usually not be achieved until later.
4. Dump: Waste/improvements only have low effect and require high effort; therefore, you will probably choose the others instead. For example, it might be something that saves two minutes, but requires a whole day to make.

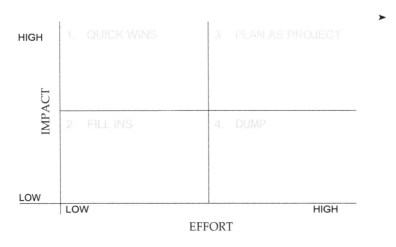

Action Plan   Finally, you agree who does what and when. It must be specific, but it might be that one of you are to investigate something before the next meeting. It might also be that two employees together make a proposal for a new procedure. You will not have time for a detailed discussion on how to solve a problem. The person in charge of the meeting must stop such a discussion. Fifteen minutes is not a long time, and energy disappears if you just prolong the meeting.

---

150 IMPROVEMENTS A YEAR

If you adopt and achieve three improvement suggestions every week, you will have achieved 150 improvement suggestions in a year. That is an OK achievement!

The suggestions you don't have time to discuss must be dealt with at the following week's meeting. It may be easier to make suggestions than to implement them. If the suggestion is to make changes on some gates, you need an employee who has the time to do it. It might therefore be a good idea to decide a maximum number of improvement suggestions every week.

When a suggestion is written on the action plan, you can throw the colored sticky notes out. Now it is on the list. Give the adopted suggestions consecutive numbering. Write the numbers on the action plan, and use them to sum up the number of achieved suggestions. It helps illustrate how much actually happens.

NO. IMPROVEMENTS SUGGESTED	
NO, IMPROVEMENTS IMPLEMENTED	

The Positive Dialogue   At the board meetings, it is important to have a positive dialogue – also in the body language. Your body language must express the same as your verbal language.

In Lean, errors are source of improvement. Therefore, rejoice every time an error becomes known. Then you can learn from it and be better next time. If an employee fears scolding because he has made a mistake, he will not tell you about it. And then you can't help it happening again.

If an employee has forgotten to close a gate, allowing the animals to collect, you can discuss how to avoid it another time. Because it will happen again. You can agree to go to the spot and look at the problem. We call it "Go-Look-See".

A few guidelines for dialogue during the board meeting:

- All things have a good and a bad side – also errors: What can we learn from the error?
- Quickly turn negative to positive: "What can I do better?" Instead of "He forgot to do ..." It may be that the instruction was not updated.
- Opportunity to praise: "Super, that you noticed the defective chain in the machine".
- Always avoid irony and sarcasm.

> **PRAISING IS BETTER THAN SCOLDING**
>
> Employees grow with praise and shrink with criticism.

- If you want to criticize anybody, do it when alone together.
- Do not use the board meeting to be admonishing to employees or conditions that annoy you. It may be tempting when everybody is together, but it destroys the idea of the meeting. If you are unhappy with something, act immediately toward the employee you are not satisfied with.

7.1.2.4 THE ROLE OF THE PERSON IN CHARGE OF THE MEETING

The chairperson must ensure a good and efficient conduct of the meeting. It is important that all participants can make themselves heard. There must be a good atmosphere making everyone feel comfortable and wanting to bring out ideas and improvement suggestions.

It is a good idea to take turns being in charge of board meetings. For example, you can have a month each. It helps everyone to become active in the improvement work. It may be uncomfortable for some to stand in front of an audience, but then you can use courses or a coach to prepare you for the task.

Here is a checklist of the chairperson's tasks:

Before the Meeting

- Create an overview of what was agreed at the last meeting.
- Talk to colleagues in the days before the meeting, and motivate them to come up with waste or improvement suggestions.
- You may arrange with colleagues to go into the barn to have a look, if there is a specific waste or improvement suggestion. Maybe a suggestion to change a gate requires you to have a look at it.

During the Meeting

- Conduct the meeting so that everyone is concentrated and attentive. If necessary, ask directly if someone is hiding. Observe time.
- Make sure that everybody understands what is said – in particular if you speak more languages.
- Be acknowledging to all suggestions.
- Avoid negativity and attacking each other if production has been tricky. Use errors for positive learning, for example "What can we do to avoid recurrence?"
- Make sure as an owner to play your role properly: Decision making without dominance.

After the Meeting

- Follow up on the agreements; for example, continue talking to the colleague who came up with an improvement suggestion, to ensure elaboration of the suggestion.
- Evaluate the meeting with a person from the outside – what went well, and what can be done better?

Question:
We cannot have a board meeting with everyone at the same time, because we work in three shifts, and I cannot ask them to come 15 minutes in the morning. How do we solve that?

Answer:
You have to give board meetings a high priority. They are decision-making meetings; decisions on improved procedures, changes, goals and so on are being taken. If they want influence, they have to be there. And if you want them to contribute with suggestions, you must pay them to come. You also have an interest in the fact that all three teams work according to the same principle. In addition, you do not create any improvements without participation from everyone in the team. If they cannot come in the morning, you might find another time of the day. You only need a meeting once a week. Arable workers can participate over the phone.

Question:
How far in the future can we make deadlines?

Answer:
Max. one to two weeks to avoid declarations of intent. Maybe a suggestion requires a major readjustment and consequently lies in the future. Then you can decide that it should be included in next year's work plan, or you create a project plan. As a result, the note is no longer on the board, but has been sent to the headquarters.

Question:
How do we accomplish all improvement suggestions?

Answer:
It is important that all suggestions adopted by the group are achieved. It is very demotivating with a lot of loose ends and suggestions, which came to nothing. Your improvement work must be closely related to your goal.

Question
How do we keep the board meetings going?

Answer:
Leadership support is needed and the fact that management is prioritizing Lean work. This means that board meetings and improvement work must be entered into the work plan, so no one is prevented from attending. You need to make the board meeting an important decision meeting where employees will feel cheated if they cannot participate. Do not move decisions to other meetings – then you undermine board meetings. Moreover, do not cancel due to bustle and vacation. Run it consistently even if you are only two employees left.

Question:
Why do we have to stand?

Answer:
There are more dynamics in a standing meeting. Everybody is able to see and listen. You participate in a different way. At the same time, the standing position signals promptness without waste of time. You cannot achieve the same intensity and atmosphere if you sit down with your cups of coffee.

Question:
How do we shorten the meetings? They last too long.

Answer:
Meetings should not be used for technical debates. Only for decision making. If you disagree about a suggestion, let a couple of employees investigate it before the next meeting. It is a waste of time if everybody must listen to something that can be dealt with by two. Be consistent with the 15 minutes' board meeting time. Gradually, as you train, you will get there. Also, remember to start punctually every time – regardless of whether everyone has arrived.

Question:
We have so many improvement suggestions, what do we do?

Answer:
Great that it bubbles. Ensure a good priority, so you first take the ones with highest impact and lowest effort. Make a good planning of the slightly more demanding suggestions so everyone can see what's going to happen and when.

7.1.3 PDCA

PDCA is a problem-solving model, which you can use to make continuous improvement. It is also called the improvement wheel.

PDCA stands for

- Plan: Plan a test of an improvement.
- Do: Test the improvement, preferably in a limited area.
- Check: Does the improvement work as intended?
- Act: Implement the improvement in practice and make a standard for it.

The improvement wheel helps improve standards and work processes. Spin the wheel several times, for each time there is an improvement of the standard. You will learn something new every time.

7.1.3.1 YOU CAN ACHIEVE

- **Good systematics.** You can achieve good systematics in the way you work with improvement suggestions.
- **Visibility.** The treatment of a suggestion will have various steps. With the circle, everybody knows where in the process we are.
- **Development of best method.** By working systematically with planning and testing you will find the best solution instead of just the first solution.

Using a clear model makes it easier to understand for everyone. If an employee makes a suggestion, he might be disappointed that it is only going to be tested for a week if he had expected it to be implemented straight away. But knowing the systematic way to find the best solution will enable him to understand.

You probably already use the model when making a new tool, for example, you weld a sheet, test it, change a bit and try again.

7.1.3.2 HOW TO DO

Plan   You discuss a problem or an improvement suggestion. How do you approach it? What is needed? How to do it? Maybe you will analyze the problem to ensure the right approach. You then arrive at a plan for what you want to do.

Do   You decide to try the suggestion on a few animals or a limited area for a certain period. Then you will see if it works. You agree on the time to spend on it. Sometimes it is a small thing that you can implement immediately, but you must still go through the rest of the PDCA circle.

Check   When some time has elapsed, you check if the change has had the expected effect. Was it an improvement? If not, you take another turn in the wheel, that is you change something and test again.

Act   If the improvement/the suggestion works as expected, you implement it as a new regular procedure. You need to make a new standard operating procedure (SOP) or a new agreement to implement it.

The circle never ends. The idea is that you constantly find new and better ways to do things, exactly as the fifth Lean principle describes.

BETTER FEED QUALITY WITH PDCA

At a farm, they had a problem with the roughage. There was too much waste because poor feed was brought in to the cows. Several employees mixed the feed, and there were several ways to take out and sort the feed. Sometimes a lot of plastic was removed to save time on covering.

They agreed to make a standard for taking out and mixing the feed. To find the best method, they used the PDCA circle.

Plan: The employees started to talk about what the problem really was, and how the mixing should be carried out properly. They talked it through carefully and took pictures of how it should be done.

Do: The new standard was tested for a month.

Check: After a month, they checked whether waste had been reduced. They changed the procedure a little because they had seen a way to improve. Moreover, some of the employees wanted a clearer definition of some of the process steps.

Act: They made a new SOP from the new standard they had agreed on.

Question:
It sounds like a cumbersome method. If new suggestions come up, we should not initiate them as soon as possible, then?

Answer:
It is a waste of time, if the new method is not 100% good. Usually, something can be changed for the better. Therefore, it is a good thing to test the method before implementing it. For example, it may happen that you find a solution to a machine problem. But by working with the PDCA circle, you come up with another solution where you do not have to use the machine at all.

Question:
When we have tested a new suggestion and find that it doesn't work, do we just go back to the old system?

Answer:
You need to figure out why it doesn't work, and then come up with suggestions how to correct it. Development often occurs in small spurts with lots of trials that are not successful. Suddenly one day it works, but still development must continue.

> **Question:**
> If something works well, why change it?
>
> **Answer:**
> Development only occurs if you make changes. If you test the improvement suggestion on a smaller scale, you will see whether there is improvement before implementing it.

7.1.4 VALUE STREAM MAPPING

Value stream mapping is a mapping of all process steps, both value-adding and non-value-adding. The purpose is to create a common understanding of the current situation and to spot waste so that it can be removed.

7.1.4.1 YOU CAN ACHIEVE

- **Reduce waste**, which takes up too much process steps and costs money.
- **Everyone is observant** of identifying waste on the farm.
- **Greater flexibility**, because all employees know all process steps and know why and how to solve all tasks.
- **The employees start to think differently** and come up with improvement suggestions.
- **Employees are motivated**, because they are involved in creating improvement.

THE EIGHT WASTES

1. Defects
2. Overproduction
3. Waiting
4. Non-utilization of talent
5. Transport
6. Inventory
7. Motion
8. Extra processing

7.1.4.2 HOW TO DO

The Burning Platform   The first thing to do is to define the burning platform, that is your greatest challenge.

Discuss where your greatest challenge is. It is a good idea to start with value stream mapping. There may well be several value stream mappings within the same field of work. But start where you think the biggest challenge lies.

Employees must be in production when making value stream mapping

Examples of a burning platform:

- Performance is too low to meet earning goals
- Too many man-hours per produced unit
- Our costs are too high
- Enlargement requires more people, which we cannot get
- Too many animals die
- Too many accidents on the farm
- Quality of our products is too poor
- Diesel consumption too high
- We waste time on transport

THE BURNING PLATFORM

The (main) problem, which challenges the farm.

In the following example, the burning platform is that the farrowing unit produces too-small piglets. The pigs are not thriving when they are transferred to the weaning unit.

Supplier and Customer   The next step is to define the area of production you want to map. You must define beginning and end of the process in question – that is, supplier and customer.

We have here both internal supplier and internal customer. Thus, the farrowing unit is the supplier of the "seven-kg production". The seven-kg production in the weaning unit is then the customer.

Once you have agreed on the farm's burning platform and have defined the area, it is time to take a walk in the production.

Examples of internal supplier and internal customer

Supplier		Production		Customer
Farrowing unit	➡	Pigs at 7 kg	➡	Weaning unit
Weaning unit	➡	Pigs at 30 kg	➡	Finisher farm
Finisher farm	➡	Pigs at 120 kg	➡	Market

Time to "Go Gemba"   In Lean language, a walk in the production is called to "Go Gemba". Here you see how things are done and how long it takes. You can base your observations on data and registrations, but the most important thing is to use your eyes.

You all know the production and may not think it necessary to thoroughly go through it together. But you will see something else when you focus on what you do together. You will spot waste when you go through the process steps and question why you do as you do.

In addition, you can record the process on video and see it through together afterward. It may also open your eyes to potential improvements.

Mapping on Brown Paper   Put a large piece of brown paper on the wall for everyone to see.
Start by defining customer requirements, and write them on the right side. Customer requirements are what has real value for the customer. Do not think about what is or is not possible. You must think what is best for the customer in the ideal world. That is what you must strive to fulfill.

In our example, the demands of the weaning unit (the customer) is that the pigs weigh seven kg.

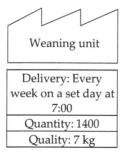

▨ Write the supplier in the left-hand side of the brown paper. The supplier here is the farrowing unit.

```
      ┌─────┐  ┌─────┐
     /      \ /      \
    /        V        \
   ┌───────────────────┐
   │                   │
   │   Farrowing unit  │
   │                   │
   ├───────────────────┤
   │ Delivery: Sun–Tue │
   ├───────────────────┤
   │ Quantity: 1300–1600│
   ├───────────────────┤
   │ Quality: 0,8–2,2 kg│
   └───────────────────┘
```

▨ Now you map the current workflow by writing on sticky notes and putting them on the brown paper. The colors of the sticky notes mean different things (see the following bullet points). Hang a poster on the wall showing the meaning of the colors.

▨ You must map the current state step by step. It is important to be very detailed because you find the waste in the detail. Example: "Fetch trough for additional milk feeding". How far do you go? How do you carry it? What is the condition of the road you go by? Do you have to wait? How long does it take? How many times do you need to go back and forth? Do you do it the same way all of you? This way you go through each processual step in the workflow and in the sequence of workflows.

▨ Write each process steps on a yellow sticky note. If there are more steps in the process, they turn into process steps that you put under the overall workflow/process.

▨ Every time you identify waste, you put a green sticky note making it clear where there are opportunities for improvement.

▨ If, during value stream mapping, an improvement suggestion is spontaneously put forth, you write it on a pink sticky note. Do not deal with it during mapping, but return to it when mapping is completed.

▨ If, during mapping, disagreement arises, write an orange sticky note. Then you know that you must return to it later. However, don't stop mapping to discuss how to do things.

▨ When shifting responsibility from one person to another, you use the blue sticky notes.

MAPPING – IN PRODUCTION

Value stream mapping is best done by bringing a roll of paper, sticky notes and pens into the production environment and mapping the process there. This provides visibility and a common understanding of where there is waste.

Time Every Processual Step   When you have mapped the entire value stream, you time every single process step. Most mappings don't require very exact timing. It suffices to ask the person who does the job on a daily basis and then compare the answer to the total time consumption. If you map an exact process, for example transfer of pigs, it is a good idea, though, to time all processual steps. Here, just a few minutes make a difference.

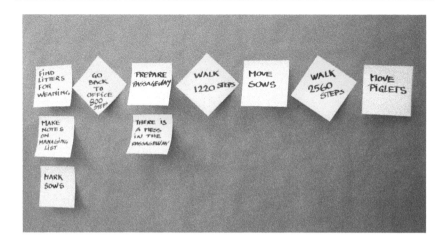

The figure shows the end of a value stream mapping in the farrowing unit You must calculate two time lapses:

- Production Lead Time: From start to finish, that is from supplier to customer
- Processing Time: The time the product is in work or the time you actually do something

For example, Lead Time for a pig, on one hand, is the time it takes the pig to be ready for the customer (grow to seven kg). Processing Time, on the other hand, is the time you actually work with the pig, feed, clean the pen, move the animals and so on. Between the two calculations, you have a mapping that can be used to optimize the total value stream. Value stream mapping provides an overview indicating where there is waste and where bottlenecks occur in the processes. In addition, you get all the processes reviewed with all employees, so that, among other things, it will be clear whether the pigs are tended to systematically or randomly. Another example could be if the growth of the pigs is decreasing for some reason.

Future State   You have mapped your current state, where many green and pink sticky notes show wastes and improvement suggestions. When you are to set your future state, you start looking at all the workflows again. This time you assume that you can dream without any restrictions. What will your value stream look like?

When you have described your future state, you calculate process and flow times again to see what can be achieved in the ideal state. A high and steady growth will certainly affect process and flow time, while still meeting customer demand of seven kg.

Change of Current State Now comes the most interesting part. You need to examine how to get from your current state to your future state. Between current state and future state, there is a gap. You have probably found many wastes and improvement suggestions in your value stream. What does it take to get to the future state, and how can you do it?

You must prioritize all your green notes dealing with waste, in relation to effect and effort.

Prioritizing and Action Plan The mapping shows the entire value stream. You have probably found many things that need changing to get to your future state. You cannot handle it at once, but you can split it into smaller steps after an implementation plan.

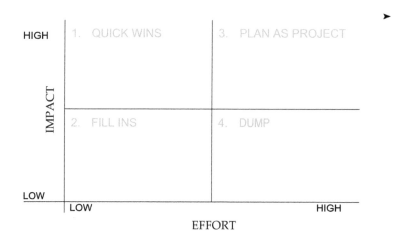

The sticky notes dealing with waste must be handled the following way:

- They are prioritized in the matrix (which we deal with in the section about board meetings)
- Deal with them one by one. If needed, make a root cause analysis, which can help you see the problem from all sides, so you continue with the right cause for the waste. What is the root cause? What solutions and improvements do you see?
- The suggestions must be taken through the PDCA circle; that will help you structure the process of testing and implementing the improvements.
- Then you write the tasks on the action plan that you choose to address. Larger things can be written in a project plan.

Activity	Deadline	Responsible
Test a new weighing procedure at weaning	25.1.	Peter
Replace water nipples in barn 4	26.1.	Paul
Meet with manager of weaning unit	23.1.	John

7.1.5 STANDARDIZATION

SOP is short for standard operating procedure, but often only the term "standard" is used. It is a step-by-step description of how to perform a task. It must ensure that a task is performed the best possible way and the same way by everybody. It can also be pictures of the wanted quality of work, for example how clean the floor should be.

Good standards are dynamic, that is they are easily adjusted if you find a better way to do the job.

Pictures and drawings are quick to "read" when you just need to find out something specific. They are also a great help for foreign employees.

The sight is our most dominant sense, and we learn and remember best through pictures, not through written or spoken words. When we get information in writing or speech, three days later we will only remember 10% of it. If a picture has been added, we will remember 65%.

Standards must hang close to where they are to be used. It is therefore a good idea to put up rails so that the SOPs can be placed near the calves, workshop, sorting room and so on.

7.1.5.1 YOU CAN ACHIEVE

- **Committed employees.** You must involve your employees when you are to describe how to perform a task and to make a standard. You must take some good professional discussions, become wiser and eventually agree how to do it.
- **Uniformity.** You can ensure that all employees carry out tasks in the same ways. No one at the farm is in doubt as to how the individual tasks should be performed.
- **Streamlining.** With a standard, you have found the best way to do it. This means that not all workers need to reinvent the wheel. The most effective way is described, and everyone can do the task straight away.
- **Saving time.** You save time when introducing new employees, and they soon get the idea because they can look up how to do the job. When the task is done correctly and efficiently the first time, you save time because you do not need to correct mistakes.

Question:
When we have mapped the value stream on brown paper and with sticky notes, I would like to enter and save it on my computer. Do you have a program for that?

Answer:
It is actually a waste of time to transfer the analysis to the PC. The most important part of value stream mapping is the process and the waste you identify. It is written on your sticky notes, which you bring along to board meetings to work with. The brown paper indicates that it is process paper, so it must be thrown out afterwards. If you want to save what it says, take some good photos of the board instead.

Question:
Are we never to implement the improvements from the square DUMP?

Answer:
They are improvements with low impact demanding high effort. Instead, you should deal with the suggestions demanding low impact with a high effect.

Question:
How do we ensure that we have defined the right burning platform?

Answer:
It must make both you and your employees realize that change is necessary.

- **Saving money.** Ignorance is a major source of errors, which are often expensive. With a SOP, you minimize the risk of employees making mistakes.

KNOWLEDGE HOUR

On the first Thursday of each month, the manager invites the entire staff for a knowledge hour/class. A new topic is introduced every month, which they are taught, discuss and make decisions on. At the end of the hour, there is a draft for a standard for the area. It is made into an SOP with pictures and hung up in the barn.

Time Schedule Knowledge Hour – SOP

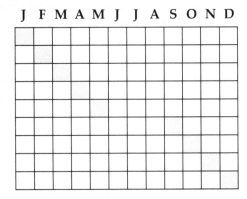

	J	F	M	A	M	J	J	A	S	O	N	D
Safety - mini loader												
Quality control of feed												
High pressure cleaner												
Our hygiene standard												
Set irrigation system												
Check driving tractors												
Hand over a machine												
Driving on the road												
Communication												

7.1.5.2 HOW TO DO

If you do not already have written standards for the procedures, start by making them. Once there are improvement suggestions at the board meetings, you can adjust the standards as you find even better ways to do things.

SUCCESS DEPENDS ON INVOLVEMENT

We are in no doubt that you are more likely to follow a standard if you have helped to make it.

You should make the standards together, and preferably one area at a time. You must all be able to relate to them and use them before proceeding to the next area. To achieve this, it is important that the employees closest to the process contribute to making the standard.

All steps/processes involved in the task must be included. Here is an example of daily maintenance of the tractor before it starts working.

Lubricating the front bucket every Monday	
Check water on the cooler before you leave	
Check engine oil before you leave	

EASY TO DO IT RIGHT

At a large cattle farm, a full-time employee looked after the calves. She was very committed and focused on calf mortality and health. She did not, however, focus on work rationalization and systematics. "You have to spend time to care for calves", was her conviction.

She had developed her own systems with colostrum. Through a smooth transition, the calves were fed different types of milk – and each calf received individual care following an assessment of appetite and so on.

It was complicated, and hence mistakes were made when she had time off. For example, the field hand who replaced her on weekends had to assess whether colostrum after three days in the refrigerator was good enough for the calves. He also had to assess whether it was 30 or 40 degrees in temperature when he came back to the bath – for perhaps the third and fourth time. For each weekend, long notes with instructions were issued.

They had to establish fixed procedures, but it was difficult to convince the regular calf handler. However, it was tried, and only then she could see that the fixed procedures ensured the same care both weekdays and weekends. It became easy to do it right.

Question:
I'm afraid my employees will think I underestimate them. It is a bit like a comic strip. How do I get beyond that?

Answer:
The most important thing is to involve them in making the procedure. It challenges most people to write down what they do and, with others, agree on the best method. The pictures make it quicker to grasp, and they ensure that you understand things the same way.

Question:
Is it not best to make SOPs in the employee's own language?

Answer:
The procedure must be dynamic, enabling you to discuss it and adjust it when you find improvements. Thus, you should write it in your every-day language. The text should be short, and the pictures will help you remember. If you write in two languages, do it in the same section, so you are certain it says the same thing.

Question:
Will it not deprive the employees of initiative when everything they are to do is described in detail?

Answer:
The employees must write the procedure. If they find a better method later, it is good. They then have to test the new method, and if they find that it works, they will adjust the SOP. The basis of all improvement is that you know exactly what you do now.

7.1.6 5S

5S is a system for getting things in order. It is called 5S after the Japanese names Seiri (Sort), Seiton (Set in Order), Seiso (Shine), Seiketsu (Standardize) and Shitsuke (Sustain).

1. Sort
2. Set in Order
3. Shine
4. Standardize
5. Sustain

5S describes how a field of work can be organized without mess and how it can be maintained like that. The decision-making process is a dialogue between the people involved, and it must be based on a clear understanding between them as to how they wish it to be. That is crucial to making them have ownership of the cleanup and the new standard.

SIMPLE TOOL FOR SYSTEM AND ORDER

Do you sometimes look for things because you cannot remember where they were last placed? Are you frustrated when you find the spare part you were looking for last week after you had to buy a new one because you could not find it?

5S is a simple tool that here and now can save time and frustration and help create system and order.

FULL FOCUS ON TASK SOLUTION

We know the alternative. It is the usual declaration of intent that "Now we must help one another to keep order". It just doesn't happen, and it often ends with admonition and irritation. With 5S you work with a completely fixed five-point system. Systematics ensure your concentration is on solving the tasks rather than discussing who is to decide. You make a system and together make sure to update it. It is brilliant, and that is why it works.

7.1.6.1 YOU CAN ACHIEVE

- **Saving time**, because you don't have to look for things.
- **Less space requirements**, because only the important things are left – the rest is gone.
- **Better organization of the workplace**, you have what you need right at hand. It is located right for the task.
- **Better working environment**, because of tidiness, less waste of time and less irritation.
- **Better safety** – all things have a "home", nothing is in an inappropriate place.

7.1.6.2 HOW TO DO

Choose a minor area where you make 5S. Start by defining the tasks in and features of the area. For example, production areas and storage must be separate. Then go through all the steps, and get the standard to work before moving on to the next area.

5S can be made everywhere on the farm:

- In a section of the barn
- In the workshop
- In the store house
- In the office
- In the mailbox
- In the castration box

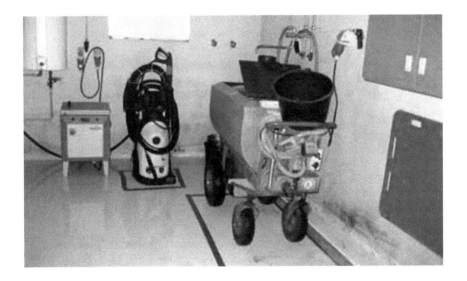

Each tool has its place in the calf kitchen. The marks on the floor indicate where each thing belongs

Sort You start by sorting the essential from the insignificant. Move it all out of the work area. All employees are equipped with green, yellow and red sticky notes.

- Green sticky notes are put on things you use every day, and which must be close at hand.

- Yellow sticky notes are put on items that you use occasionally or rarely. They may well be in another room or a remote storage.
- Red sticky notes are put on items that you never use or will probably never use again. Decide whether you want to sell them or throw them out.

Then the team discuss the location of the green and yellow items.

Examples   A cattle trimmer is not needed in the milking parlor. It is used a couple of times a year and should not be a nuisance in the milking parlor every day.

Don't store a stack of pallets where you work. Only keep the ones you use right now.

Red Tag Area   You will encounter some things that you don't really know whether to keep or throw out. Therefore, mark a red tag area where you can put those things. Then after some time you will know if you need those things or the owner should assess whether to throw them out or sell them.

Set in Order   When you have sorted, everything must be set in order, systematically. It must be done logically, enabling everybody to find what he or she needs.

Example   Everything you need to prepare the machines must be assembled – possibly on a wagon so you can take it round to the machines. Examples of this are sprinkler heads, oil, grease, measuring instruments and so on. Mark the location of everything, making it clear if something is missing.

> There must be a place for everything, and everything must be in place.

Shine   Place everything so that it is easy to clean. Do not place anything directly on the floor, and do not leave anything that needs to be moved before you can clean. Make a standard for how tidy and clean office/workshop should be. Make a fixed plan for cleaning, with both time and responsibility.

Standardize To ensure that system and order in the workshop becomes a permanent state, it is necessary to make a standard indicating how the workshop should look. Once you have placed the items as agreed, take pictures of the correct organization and hang them in the workshop. This way you enable  replacement workers to work according to the standard and hand over the workshop in the desired state.

Sustain Self-discipline is both the hardest and the most important element. Once you have introduced 5S in an area, it must remain that way. You must be aware that the newly acquired order is not sliding without you noticing it. Since you are in the area on a daily basis, you may not see it. This is why pictures are so good. You must make an audit every week. Fill in a form in which you give marks to the appearance of the working area. Bring the ratings to the board meetings and hang them up – both when things are OK, and when you need to pull yourselves together. It must be agreed what triggers corrective action. For example, you can agree that a score of 2 and below requires a common cleanup on the following Friday.

Weekly 5S audit

No	Description	Yes (x)	No (x)	Corrective action	Resp.
1	Are all activities performed after last week's cleaning plan?	x			
2	Are all tools placed according to standard?		x		
3	Are all tools/all facilities placed in fixed, marked places?	x			
4	Is the work area according to standard?	x			
5	Is the floor tidy and according to standard?		x		
6	Are whiteboards tidy?	x			
7	Has an action plan been made for last week's deviations in this audit?	x			

How are 5S Audits Used? Every week, you go through the area and answer "Yes" or "No" to the questions.

If the answer to a question is "No", you must add a corrective action. The number of "Yes" is read and plotted on the graph.

Calving as an Example   Many employees have tried looking for the OB (Obstetric chains) chains) and then after a long search found them in a bucket in a corner – very dirty.

With 5S it is different. Here the idea is that everything used in the calving section must be nearby.

If you do not have the opportunity to have things ready at hand or in a closet at the calving area, you can make toolboxes with items that you use for calving. You bring the toolbox along when you go to the calving cow. Then the tools are always at hand, and you do not have to go back for anything.

It is important that every single item has a "home" where it belongs. So when the toolbox has been brought to a calving, it returns home when calving is over. Then it is ready for the next calving.

If things have a "home", it is very conspicuous if they are suddenly not there. Here you need self-discipline to quickly get things back in order.

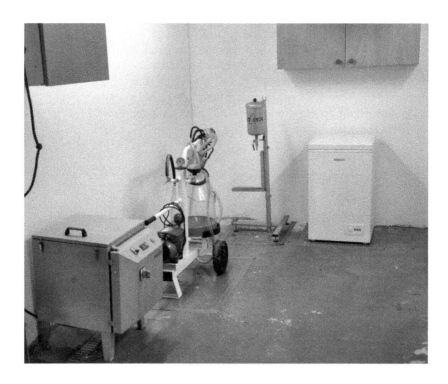

The calving kitchen is designed so that the allocation of colostrum is rational

Before

Everyone helps sorting

After

Everything is taken out on the floor

Now we sort out. What do we use daily, weekly, annually?

End result

Question:
Where can we use 5S?

Answer:
5S can be used everywhere: in the workshop, the barn, the machine house, the feed storage shed, the alleys, the office, the mailbox on the tractor and so on.

Question:
Who should participate in making 5S?

Answer:
Those who work in the affected area. Everyone who works and comes in the area (one would like to find things again). It is all about ownership and promoting the team spirit by making a joint effort to keep everything tidy.

Question:
My employees still make a mess, even after we have implemented 5S – what do we do?

Answer:
It may be because things are not placed appropriately. If cleaning is awkward, it will not work. If not ALL items have their own place, they will be placed randomly.

Nevertheless, something indicates that they don't respect audits and joint agreements. Have a talk about it using the questions, We have made 5S, how do you think it works? How do you think we can make it work? Pictures showing what it should look like may also be beneficial.

7.1.7 KANBAN

Kanban means "signal" in Japanese. It is a method of managing purchases so that nothing is missing or bought more than necessary for stock. A Kanban-card sends a signal to either supplier or purchaser when filling up is needed.

Kanban is also used in production to signal what needs to be produced when, and how much. A Kanban system is used to only produce what is needed rather than filling internal stocks.

7.1.7.1 YOU CAN ACHIEVE

- **Demand-controlled stock.** If demand increases, the Kanban-card will ensure that more items are ordered. If demand drops, only sufficient items are ordered from the supplier.
- **Low stock level.** No more than is decided beforehand will be refilled. Stocks are typically reduced by at least 20%.
- **Visual system.** The Kanban-card communicates in writing, so there are no oral agreements of the type "I'll remember to order".
- **Systematics.** You don't need to remember a lot of unnecessary things. When all purchases are systematized and handled almost automatically on a fixed day of the week, you can pay attention to other things.

7.1.7.2 HOW TO DO

1. Start by identifying the places at the farm where it would be obvious to use Kanban-cards. It could be for
   - Wipers
   - Fluorescent lamps
   - Tools
   - Syringes
   - Detergents
   - Soap
   - Transponders
   - Marking colors
   - Spare parts for machines
   - Dressings
   - Various creams
   - Toilet paper
   - Medicine
   - Minerals and vitamins

2. For each item, make a card that can be laminated.
3. Place the card among the last items in a stock, for example on top of the last packet.
4. When you take the last packet, you put the card in a holder on the notice board.
5. On an agreed weekday, the purchaser takes all cards from the holder and orders new items.
6. When the goods are delivered and stored, put the card on top of the last packet again.

Whether the card is to be exactly placed on the last packet is determined by the daily consumption and length of delivery time. If there is one week's delivery time on an item, there must be enough for at least one week's consumption + buffer.

With the Kanban-card you write all relevant information on the item. It makes it so much easier to order new items. Necessary data is

- Where to order: Contact email address and/or phone number
- How many units to order
- Product code
- Possibly the person responsible for ordering the new product

How many units to order per time depends on the agreement you have with the supplier and the policy that you have on your farm.

PRODUCT (No. and description)	QUANTITY TO ORDER (Calculated from consumption and delivery time)
MILKING GLOVES CODE: 1342 SIZE, LARGE	**50 PACKS** of 100 pieces
SUPPLYER (Name and phone no. and email)	DELIVERY TIME (Hours or days and day of the week)
DAVIDSWAY.COM code: ABC321	**14 DAYS**

Example of Kanban-card

Question:
Should the same person order all items?

Answer:
The best thing is to let the people who work with the goods order them. That way you avoid the extra stage. At the Kanban-card you write everything the person needs to know to place the order.

Question:
Why not just write it on a board?

Answer:
The Kanban-card ensures that orders are placed on time, and it saves some time that all information is on the card. The card is also located exactly where you take the goods.

Question:
When employees order goods, you cannot negotiate the price.

Answer:
You may do that when once a year, you negotiate the price of your entire consumption of goods.

7.1.8 TPM

TPM means Total Productive Maintenance. It is a maintenance method that comprises preventive maintenance with the purpose of avoiding waste, stops and defects. At the same time, it implicates the Lean mindset of continuous improvements.

GOAL: ZERO ACUTE BREAKDOWNS

- 0 defects
- 0 downtime
- 0 waste
- 0 accidents

Today, you may call the blacksmith or a fitter when a machine has downtime. Typically, it takes one day to get the spare part home and maybe another day to get the machine repaired. In the meantime, production has stood still and may have given rise to several unfortunate influences in other sections.

If you use the elements in TPM, you will avoid this because you have done preventive maintenance, you have trained your own employees to take responsibility and carry out repairs. You may even have the spare part at home.

As with all Lean tools, involvement of employees is central. Thus, it is not just a systematization of the work to maintain the production apparatus. It is as much a system that puts the maintenance responsibility on the employees who work with it on a daily basis.

With TPM, you also work on continuous improvement, all along enabling you to achieve a better use of the capacity and lower costs.

In concrete terms, the employees contribute to ensuring better utilization of the material. You measure capacity, discuss how the equipment can be used better, educate people to do something themselves, organize continuous improvements and so on.

COUNT ON THREE YEARS

Typically, it takes at least three years to introduce the TPM concept if you want a culture change that causes employees to think of improvements daily and take responsibility for their own equipment.

Michael Vaag,
Valcon Consutancy A/S.

When the employees who work with the equipment on a daily basis are in charge of maintenance, you can

- **Save waiting time** because you do not have to call a fitter so often.
- **Make better use of capacity** because the equipment doesn't have so many breakdowns.
- **Spare machines**, because you don't need the overcapacity when everything is running stable and without breakdowns.
- **Get a lower blacksmith bill**, because preventive maintenance is introduced.

AUDI: EFFICIENCY 20% UP

"In one year, our press shops has provided 20 percent more items due to the TPM-system".

Axel Bienhaus,
Presswerk AUDI AG (www.forcam.de)

Employees are educated in maintenance and take responsibility to perform it.

BETTER UTILIZATION CAN SAVE PURCHASES

A farmer said that his production system was maximized and that there were one or more bottlenecks on the farm, that is, machines or sections with too little capacity to cope with enlargement. "We have maximized capacity", he said.

By an immediate look at the farm and the number of employees, it sounded right. The employees were constantly busy. Thus, an employee was involved in hitching an implement to the tractor and driving with it, switching to another variant, retrieving material and – when occasionally the machine had stopped – requesting assistance from a colleague. In addition, the machine set was idle during breaks.

So, "the capacity is maximized" was not quite true when it came to this machine set. Perhaps, therefore, it was a wrong decision to buy larger capacity because an estimation of overall equipment efficiency (OEE) could indicate some better options for utilizing capacity. Instead, they should change some workflows.

TPM can be used on all equipment/machines:

- Tractors, combine harvesters
- Skid-steer
- Telehandler
- Trailers and implements
- Robots
- Curtains/ventilation

The Six Major Losses in TPM

When a machine is not running, a loss occurs. You can divide the losses into six main types, namely,

1. Breakdown
2. Adjustments
3. Idling
4. Reduced speed
5. Defects
6. Start-up

The table shows examples of losses from a carousel and a combine harvester.

	Example from a carousel	Example from a combine harvester
1. Breakdown of machines and equipment	The carousel is idle due to a defect in the electrical system.	The auger has stopped, and the combine harvester stands still.
2. Setup, rearrangement and adjustment of the equipment	If many bucket cows in a row, the equipment must be rearranged.	The combine harvester must be set for a new crop; this requires adjustment of threshing cylinder, blower and sieves.
3. Idling and minor stops	Some places cannot be used because the cluster is in disorder. The carousel stops when a cow is to be treated.	The crop is wet, and the grain must be pushed manually to the auger in the grain tank.
4. Reduced speed of installations and equipment	The speed is reduced due to dirty udders. Other jobs during milking, i.e. treatment of diseases.	The combine harvester runs at reduced speed due to worn knives.
5. Errors, defects and work to be redone	Some cows are not properly milked on all glands due to incorrect vacuum. Kicks off without anyone discovering it. Idle milking.	The threshing cylinder has a defect beater, so the crop is not properly threshed.
6. Start-up and running-in	The carousel stands still while shifting between newly calved and other cows.	The combine harvester stands still while the new beater is mounted.

7.1.8.2 HOW TO DO

It is important that the TPM work is carried out systematically according to a particular model and with the involvement of all employees. Herein lies the difference to other maintenance programs. Systematics also make it easier to maintain the improvements.

Follow these six steps:

Step 1: Involvement and Commitment

What:

- To begin with, leader and manager must agree on what is needed.
- Organization and roles: Choose a person responsible for the project and provide him/her with the competencies to carry it through.

Note:

At a large farm, there may be different employees responsible for internal and field mechanization. If a TPM is to be made on the internal machines, the person responsible for the barn may be in charge.

Step 2: Measurement and Education

What:

- Teach your employees what TPM and OEE is (see the following point about measurement).
- Measure OEE with the employees who work with the relevant machines.
- Start with board meetings and cultivate the improvement culture.

Note:

You should know OEE of all machines – that is what is their max. capacity, and to what extent is it utilized? Where and how big is the possible waste?

Step 3: Visibility

What:

- Everybody must know the current situation. Use assessment form, OEE measurement and so on.
- Goal for the future – "How do we want it?"

Note:
For example, use the assessment form to discuss your present status and your vision for the area.

Step 4: Pilot Project

What:

- Select a type of machine to implement TPM.
- Make a TPM group – for example, one of the employees in the barn, together with the typical repairer.
- Use board meetings to involve everybody.

Note:
It must be a defined area to learn the method. This may be the ventilation system. If you choose something where breakdowns affect everyone, it gives more attention.

Step 5: Improvements

What:

- The TPM group works in TPM workshops, that is, making new standards.
- Improvements and changed work routines are standardized.
- Measurement and visualization of improvements – remember to celebrate improvements!

Note:
For example, if there has been a breakdown of the ventilation system due to wear, preventive maintenance procedures may be a new standard. Alternatively, it may be educating an employee to perform the most common repairs.

Step 6: Deployment of TPM

What:

- You make a plan for when to make TPM on all other machines.
- You must make continuous follow-up and improvements (Kaizen).

Note:
The plan must be realistic, for example with new machine type every six months or quarterly.
If it gets too hard to keep the plan, you will drop it.

7.1.8.3 MEASURING IS NECESSARY

When you start using TPM, measurements are important. Using figures to indicate how machine capacity is utilized will make you more aware of improvement opportunities. You should measure OEE and TEEP.

OEE: Utilization of Machine Capacity in Relation to Scheduled Time   OEE means Overall Equipment Efficiency and can be translated into "machine utilization".

OEE indicates how good you are at utilizing the capacity of a machine/equipment within the time you have scheduled to use it.

Do not confuse idle time with downtime. Idle time could be the time when the combine harvester is scheduled to stand still, whereas downtime means stops at times when the combine harvester was scheduled to harvest but doesn't.

TEEP: The Effective Performance of the Machine in Relation to Calendar Time   TEEP means Total Effective Equipment Performance. It is an expression of machine performance compared to 24 hours year-round.

Where OEE measures the efficiency of a machine in relation to scheduled running time, TEEP measures the running time of a machine in relation to calendar time, that is 365 days of the year, round the clock. That is an interesting figure when you are to assess your machine strategy or crop strategy, for example when having to choose the size of the header and choose the sorts.

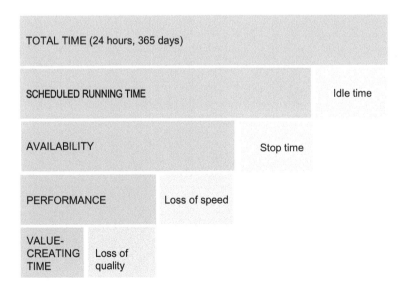

Measuring OEE It is important to emphasize that it is the machine to be measured – not the employee.

You measure by registering the "opening hours" of the machine, that is how many hours the machine is scheduled to drive in 24 hours. In addition, you measure all the stops that occur while driving, such as tool change, items to/from the machine, maintenance, breaks and so on. Low speed is included in terms of how much is being produced, while quality is included in terms of measuring approved items in relation to total production. All hours can be registered in a spreadsheet where OEE is calculated.

Registration also shows which type of stops causes the largest production losses. This gives inspiration to develop suggestions for improvement.

Measure when you initiate TPM and later, once in a while, to see what effect your improvements have had.

OEE is calculated the following way:

- Availability (A): time in operation/time available
- Performance (P): produced items/maximum number of items
- Quality (Q): approved items/number of produced items

Calculation: OEE = Machine Availability x Performance x Quality

OEE is thus the productive time in relation to the total scheduled production time. In this way, a percentage shows how much time a machine produces good items compared to the total time the machine is in operation.

What is your status?

Level 1	• Equipment is used until it breaks • All maintenance is carried out by technicians • Users are not trained in maintenance • No routine checks on the equipment • Maintenance is recorded sporadically • Preferable not to stop for preventive maintenance (PM) • Production facilities and machinery are messy and dirty	If you are on level one, start by figuring out how you want it.	Notes
Level 2	• Users know the possibilities for PM • Technicians make periodic checks • Important machines are designated as suitable for PM • Checklists for PM are made, and users are trained • PM will be performed	If you are on level two, go for the goal "Zero sudden breakdowns".	
Level 3	• Users are the first to detect abnormal things. They have the primary responsibility to take care of the equipment • The three most common causes of disturbances – dirt, poor lubrication and improper use – are all eliminated • Improvement groups work with PM • Spare parts and materials are easily accessible • Maintenance logs are available for each machine	If you are on level 3, no breakdown should occur because of the most common causes.	
Level 4	• Users make daily routine checks and lubrication. They use 5S • Sudden breakdowns don't happen anymore • Improvement measures are ongoing to find the root causes of • Breakdowns • Unstable operation of machinery • Poor training	If you are on level 4, no minor stops should occur due to equipment and machinery failure.	
Level 5	• Users are well trained in PM activities and constantly strive to find reasons for possible defects • All identified improvement options are implemented • PM runs efficiently on all machines • No errors occur during production • Reorganization takes place without the need to discard anything • All running times are as scheduled	If you are on level 5, the equipment utilization rate is 95% or more.	

An Example: Automatic Feeding System

- **Availability** means the time a machine runs by the scheduled time. In this example, a feed plant is scheduled to run 4 × 3 hours = 720 minutes/day. During the four feedings, there are 6 unplanned stops totaling 42 minutes (an average for a representative period).

  Scheduled time: 720 minutes
  Available time: 720 − 42 = 678 minutes
  Availability: 678/720 = 94%

- **Performance** means how much the machine produces in relation to calculated production. In the example, the automatic feeding system can feed 200 animals per hour or 3.3 animals/minute, but because of reduced speed, vacant pens and fewer animals per section, only 180 animals are fed per hour, equivalent to 3 animals/minute. The calculation then looks as follows:

  Available time: 678 minutes = 2257 animals
  Actual performance: 3 animals/minute = 2034 animals
  Performance: 2034/2257 = 90%

- **Quality** means how many of the units performed by the machine are of an OK quality – that is how many should not be discarded. It may be uneven feeding or mixing. Let us say that the quality here is 95%.

The automatic feeding system capacity utilization, OEE is now: 94% × 90% × 95% = 80%

The automatic feeding system capacity utilization in relation to 24 hours, TEEP is (12 × 365)/24 × 365) × 80% = 40%. You can also call it value-creating time.

Question:
I find it difficult to delegate responsibility and maybe risk not getting it done the way I want it. What do I do?

Answer:
You have to let go if you are to make other people committed. You must visualize the goals so that your employees know where they are going – and then you must be confident that you get there. It may well be in a different way than you had chosen, but if the goal is reached, it should not matter.

Question:
You also have board meetings in TPM. What is the difference between those and the other board meetings?

Answer:
TPM board meetings only include employees working with the current machines. You can set up an overall board for all machines or a smaller board at each machine, where you review target management, improvement suggestions, maintenance plans and so on. For example, it is not relevant to talk about the milking carousel in the machine house, so it depends on which machines are included.

Question:
It is not relevant if you have a service agreement, is it?

Answer:
TPM is used both to increase capacity when the machine runs and to ensure fewer and shorter stops. The more you can do yourselves and the more you can avoid stops, the better service agreement you can negotiate. Maybe you can do without it?

7.1.9 SMED

SMED is a tool for reducing changeover times. SMED means "Single-Minute Exchange of Die". You may also say "Changeover in less than ten minutes". The abbreviation states that you would like to replace a sieve, nozzle or tool in a few minutes to waste as little time as possible.

The most well-known picture of perfect SMED is the way pit stops function at motor races. It is based on preparation and training so that four wheels can be changed in less than 2.5 seconds, while windows are cleaned, and fuel tanked.

Agriculture needs changeover in a number of situations:

- The switch to milking hospital cows requires changeover. If you milk hospital cows first, disinfection and other changeovers are required before you milk the healthy cows.
- Replacing tools on tractors.
- Packing another vegetable or plant on the same packing machine.
- Lifting plants in a new field.

7.1.9.1 YOU CAN ACHIEVE

- **Larger capacity and saved working hours**. Shorter changeover times mean that machines can produce more. At the same time, employees become more efficient.
- **Less machine hours**. Machines perform when they run. There is less idle and wasted time on the machines

7.1.9.2 HOW TO DO

You probably think that you are as efficient as possible. SMED is not a tool that can create improvement by pressing a button. However, by working with measuring, systematic improvement work and training, you can make improvements together.

There are seven formal steps in a SMED process:

1. **Map What You Do Today**
   a. Video record the changeover and go through it together.
2. **Divide Time Consumption into Internal Changeover Time and External Changeover Time**

a. Internal changeover time: The time when the machine stands still while you readjust. If first you must go and fetch tools or other items, the stop will be longer than if you had had everything ready beforehand or when the machine was running. The internal changeover time must be reduced as much as possible.

b. External changeover time: The actual time it takes to convert the machine for the next task. Meanwhile the machine can run – with reduced production, however.

3. **Find Improvement Suggestions**, which move internal time to external time. It may be to take out, prepare and so on. You can prepare everything, enabling the machine to start as soon as it has reached the next field.

4. **Streamline the Remaining Internal Activities** by simplifying them: Use 5S, make standards and so forth. Perhaps you should place tools and equipment differently. You may use value stream mapping to bring out good improvement suggestions. First, take the improvements that cost no money.

5. **Streamline the External Activities** the same way.

6. **Make a New Standard and Try it Out**. Use the PDCA circle to systematize it.

7. **Repeat the Process** with a new video recording and time measurement. There will be more improvements every time.

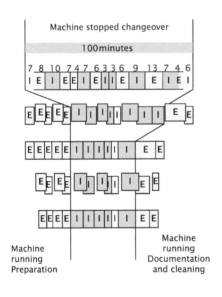

The figure shows changeover with four rounds of SMED. Changeover time is reduced, and especially internal time – when the machine stands still – has been reduced.

I: Internal time

E: External time

PREPARATION MEANT LARGER CAPACITY

A dairy farm with 4000 cows had a milking rotary with 80 stalls. They milked three times a day, and the rotary was in use 22–23 hours every day. They replaced liners after 2500 milkings, thus changing every 16 days.

It took them four minutes to replace a cluster, but it still meant five hours and 20 minutes. Even with two employees, they could not make it.

Instead of using more employees for the job, they chose to develop a method to replace liners while the rotary was running. They prepared the procedure by replacing liners in an additional set of cases. This way they were able to reduce time to replace one cluster from four minutes to one minute. Therefore, they could make it in the time between taking off a cluster and putting it on again.

SMED can be combined with the tools Standardization and 5S. Changeover is obviously faster if you find the best way, and everybody subsequently does it the same way. It is also obvious that changeover is faster if you have made a 5S, so that everything is in place and close at hand.

Question:
It does not really matter if a changeover takes five minutes more or less?

Answer:
It is most relevant to the changeovers that occur frequently, such as changing tools. There are examples that employees are going up and down the tractor and loader many times. If each changeover is also both heavy and cumbersome, you can easily waste a lot of time every day.

Question:
How do you inspire employees to do it faster?

Answer:
First, they must be involved in making the proposals. They themselves have to develop and try out the new ways to do things. It is not hard to engage people when they are involved in decision making. Moreover, most people like to work smarter.

Question:
We cannot at all agree on what is best. It easily turns into criticizing each other.

Answer:
You can make a Go-Look-See, that is together, you go and look at what happens on the spot. If possible, make a small video recording and see it through together. Together you will then find the best way.

How to Implement Lean at Your Farm

Lean is not a project with a start and end date. It is a new way of working and thinking, and a new culture must be incorporated. If you want to incorporate the new culture, you must make a long-term planning for the implementation.

8.1 HOW TO IMPLEMENT LEAN AT YOUR FARM

8.1.1 THE CURRENT STATE OF YOUR FARM

What is the status at your farm right now?
Are you ready to test if Lean can give you value?

Everything is proper and tidy, and no waste or minor storage are lying around.
☐ No, it is not like that ☐ ☐ Yes, that is how it is

Larger objects such as pallets, equipment, internal machines, etc. are located in marked places, and all walkways are free.
☐ No, it is not like that ☐ ☐ Yes, that is how it is

It is easy to keep clean because there is nothing on the floor or outside the marked areas.
☐ No, it is not like that ☐ ☐ Yes, that is how it is

All cleaning is done after a defined system, where you can see what to do when and by whom. Safety and functionality are more important than the perfect cleaning.
☐ No, it is not like that ☐ ☐ Yes, that is how it is

There are clear working instructions (standard operating procedures) that describe the various tasks of the workplace. All written instructions are updated and are used.
☐ No, it is not like that ☐ ☐ Yes, that is how it is

Employees can identify waste in production and actively participate in reducing waste in the daily work processes.
☐ No, it is not like that ☐ ☐ Yes, that is how it is

The employees in each area work systematically to make continuous improvements. It happens at daily or weekly meetings at a board.
☐ No, it is not like that ☐ ☐ Yes, that is how it is

The PDCA enhancement method is used to support employee improvement work. The leader demands concrete improvements and facilitates improvement efforts.
☐ No, it is not like that ☐ ☐ Yes, that is how it is

You work with clear goal management at boards, and all employees can see the connection between your goals on the day-to-day level to your executive goals.
☐ No, it is not like that ☐ ☐ Yes, that is how it is

You have a system for systematic maintenance of machines, and your employees are trained and instructed in preventive maintenance.
☐ No, it is not like that ☐ ☐ Yes, that is how it is

When employees find defects or other types of waste, they always bring it up at board meetings with the purpose of finding solutions and improvements. Errors will never be hidden.
☐ No, it is not like that ☐ ☐ Yes, that is how it is

If you have crossed the boxes to the left or in the center, you can create improvements by using Lean at your farm. At the same time, the statements may quite possibly tell you what kind of value you can achieve.

8.1.2 LEANSTART WITH SIMPLE TOOLS

Start by the tool best fit for your vision with Lean work. It may be an advantage to take one tool at a time and implement it well before you start on the next area or tool.

To some people, Lean can be a huge change, while others see it as logic. Therefore, it is important that everyone gets ownership of the tools and the new way of working. The most obvious tools to start with are either the board meeting or the 5S.

> **5S MEANS**
>
> - Sort
> - Set in Order
> - Shine
> - Standardize
> - Sustain

8.1.2.1 THE BOARD MEETING INVOLVES THE EMPLOYEES

The board meeting is not an easy tool. It requires a new management and communication style. Nevertheless, it is central to the work with continuous improvement and involvement of employees.

8.1.2.2 5S PROVIDES QUICK AND VISIBLE RESULTS

5S is a system for achieving tidiness and the tool that employees are most happy with. They can immediately see both the idea and the benefits. At the same time, it clearly identifies what Lean thinking really is about.

8.1.2.3 LEAN IS ALSO FOR SMALLER FARMS

The employees are an important part of Lean. Therefore, you may think that Lean is only for large farms with several employees, but a farm with a married couple or an owner + replacement worker will also be able to benefit from using Lean thinking. Some of the tools may be more relevant than others, but there are clear opportunities to create more value by implementing Lean on all farms.

8.1.3 EXPECT A TROUGH

The hype curve describes the phases you can expect to go through when you start working with Lean.

It starts with great enthusiasm because something new is happening. There is great interest and great expectations. You will reach a peak with inflated expectations where there are successes but also many mistakes. Then comes a phase of disillusionment, which gives rise to disappointment that not all expectations were met. In the next phase, some of the tools begin to work, and slowly you will see an increasing understanding. The final phase is the level of productivity you achieve in the long term.

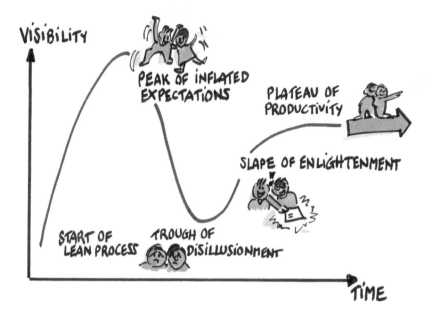

Development is initiated, on one hand, by people who think new ideas are exciting, and they like to get things started. On the other hand, the same people often find it difficult to maintain interest after some time has elapsed and there are new projects that take their focus. It is a completely natural process, and you should expect a trough.

If you are such a type, you can prepare how to get out of the hype curve again by leaving the coordinating role and responsibility for the task to another. You must acknowledge it if you are best at starting things and others are better at maintaining the process. You can also participate in a discussion group where you can talk about your position on the curve right now. Then it is easier to keep believing that it will probably start again.

8.1.4 PLAN FOR THE IMPLEMENTATION OF LEAN

As mentioned in the previous section, it is normal that there will be a drop in visibility and attention. Therefore, it is crucial that you make a plan for how to develop Lean work at the farm. Even though you start with one step at a time, you must be able to see goals and direction in the long run.

You can make Lean a culture so that it becomes your very natural way of working and thinking. You can do area by area with 5S, and you can maintain communication and improvement work with the board meetings. When you encounter a problem, you can use Lean tools to find a solution. It will continue, and you will find more and more ways to develop it. You will also have periods of crisis where everything seems to fall back to where you started. Therefore, Lean work never stops.

Next is an example of how you can carry out a full implementation of Lean. It should be seen as an inspiration for how to implement it everywhere on the farm.

HIDDEN AGENDA

The owner of a farm considered introducing board meetings. At the introduction, he was sitting at the back. He made a proposal to improve the routines but did not participate much in the debate. He was observing.

The employees were a little hesitant at first but could soon see the idea. They constructively started training, and everything seemed good.

Afterward, the owner commented that he was well pleased. Maybe now they could learn to see when routines needed to be changed. That was what he wanted to follow up on at the following meeting.

He thus pretended that with Lean he would involve the employees. In fact, he just used the tool to pull his own agenda down over their heads.

STEP 1: INTRODUCTION TO LEAN

You must have an introduction to what Lean is and what results the implementation of Lean may lead to. The participants in this introduction are initially you as the owner/leader, the leading employees and maybe your farm board of management. They must be the decision makers at your farm.

You must prepare yourselves for making a decision as to how you will handle the implementation and how many resources you will use. You will also need to assess the effect of Lean implementation on your results.

At this point, there must be time for reflection and for reading more about Lean.

STEP 2: LEAN VISION

At the next step, you must decide what you want to achieve with Lean. You must define the burning platform, and you must agree on your Lean vision.

The vision does not have to be measurable. But it must not consist of empty words, smart phrases and something that might as well have been written by your neighbor.

You must choose which tools are most suitable to fulfill your wishes.

There are more than 50 Lean tools, so it is necessary to choose which of them you want to work with.

LEAN VISIONS

Lean vision at Eastwood Estate

We want to create value without waste and involve our employees in the process – and have fun doing so!

Lean vision at Westwood Estate

We want to save working hours, improve our communication and be in control of our maintenance costs.

Lean vision at Southwood Estate

We want to be more efficient and have better teamwork between field and barn.

Lean vision at Northwood Estate

We want more tidiness on the farm, and we want to produce more with the same people.

STEP 3: TRAINING OF LEADER AND MANAGER

Leader and manager must attend a course in Lean management or change management. That will speed up the process of being good at and more comfortable with the new management style that is necessary to make the Lean culture work.

Much time can be saved by avoiding resistance from middle management.

Resistance may occur because the manager doesn't have sufficient knowledge about Lean and therefore is unable to see how to act during the change.

It is obvious that both the leader and the manager should be prepared well to teach others about the new approach. It will ensure less error and less frustration in the introductory phase.

STEP 4: ORGANIZATION AND TIME PLANNING

Designate a Lean Leader In Lean work, initiatives must be taken and followed up. Therefore, designate a Lean leader on the farm. Even if it may seem obvious to choose the owner/leader, it is not always the right choice. At least it must be a person who is enthusiastic, has the time to solve the task and is persistent. So, if the owner is the entrepreneurial type who engages in many things and continuously gets new ideas, he is not the right one for the job.

Example of Schedule	J	F	M	A	M	J	J	A	S	O	N	D
Introduction												
Lean vision												
Training of leader and middle management												
Training and workshops – employees in the barn												
• Introduction day for employees												
Training days for employees												
• Workshop with board meeting												
• Workshop with 5S												
Follow-up day for everyone												
• Workshop with value stream mapping												
Training and workshops – employees in the field												
• Workshop with TPM												
Follow-up day and status for everyone												

Divide by Teams Different teams may have different working hours and different challenges. In many cases, it is a good idea to work with Lean and continuous improvements in the groups/teams who work together on a daily basis. However, it is important that the groups learn from each other and talk together across teams. If you have multi-site production, it may be a good idea to make a team for each site.

Make a Schedule   You must decide on a schedule for the various activities. The plan must be realistic and take into account the other tasks on the farm. But as mentioned, Lean is not something you finish. Several times in the future, you will take new initiatives and adjust the plan.

In the beginning, you may need external consultants. Once you have learned to use a tool, you continue your own. Therefore, there may be more loops of introducing and training employees as you start using more tools.

STEP 5: TRAINING AND WORKSHOPS

It is now time to introduce Lean to all employees and train them in the tools. You can start with a theory day with exercises, so everyone understands what Lean is.

You will encounter resistance because you want changes, but it is our experience that employees quickly catch the idea and want to be involved. They want to work to eliminate waste, and they have a lot to offer.

It is a good idea to take one tool at a time and ensure that the new methods are incorporated. The great thing about doing things quietly is that Lean gets into the backbone and gradually turns into a culture. Moreover, it comes from below. From here, it becomes everyday life, where it is just "like we do here at the farm".

Workshop at the Farm   In a workshop, it works well to begin with a short presentation of the tool. Then it is necessary to address its practical application in the production. The first time requires introduction and guidance from outside, but otherwise you can just proceed.

STEP 6: FOLLOW-UP DAYS

You keep up the energy if you celebrate the successes. Therefore, at regular intervals, you should meet, discuss and make new plans. You must measure how much you have achieved so that everybody feels that it is worth moving on.

If the work with Lean is quiet at times, it does not necessarily have to be shut down as a failure. You will probably fall back into the old patterns. You just have to learn from it and move on.

TEN TIPS FOR SUCCESS WITH LEAN

Mogens Egegaard Sørensen, Lean Mindset and Coaching, has worked with Lean at Arla Foods, Siemens Wind Power, Nobia and Carlsberg, among others. He has ten tips to succeed with Lean in a company. The points are not in order of priority, he emphasizes.

1. **Lots of Communication.** Management must be available and follow up. It is important to create understanding and ownership of Lean work.
2. **Give Middle Management a Clear Role in the Process.** Don't fail to see them. Their role may easily become diffuse and unresolved.
3. **Employee Involvement is Crucial.** Without a massive involvement of your employees, Lean is impossible. It is the specific knowledge and commitment of your employees that implement the practical measures.
4. **Training.** There must be lots of training of both leader and employees. Lean Principles, Lean tools, project management and many other things must all be learned.
5. **Time.** Time for Lean must be created in addition to daily operations. There must be structured time for training and working with Lean.
6. **Patience.** Change takes time, and patience of all parties is a prerequisite.
7. **Involve Shop Stewards.** They are central to motivating employees and giving feedback.
8. **Ambitious Plan for Implementation.** Don't allow too much time to pass before something happens and visible results are seen.
9. **Use External/Internal Consultants.** It is crucial that there is professional and experienced help to assist with learning and developing a completely new culture of improvement.
10. **Managerial Support.** Management must have 100% focus on Lean – otherwise nothing happens. Management must hold on to the process, maintain faith in the project and follow up, follow up, follow up.

Question:
How do you end a Lean process? What is the last step?

Answer:
Among other things, Lean is about continuous improvements. So, if you have introduced a Lean culture with continuous improvement, in principle there is no last step. The will always be things to improve, also because the conditions change.

If you reach a point where you say that the culture is now introduced, and we are "Lean", then you may call it a conclusion. But as soon as you say, "We can do it now", you stop learning and creating continuous improvements.

Question:
I think it is hard to keep employees inspired. How do you do it?

Answer:
It is about being prepared as a leader. When you feel that you are going down in the trough, then focus on all that you have achieved; it gives energy. Make your goals visible, and break them down to the daily level so they are relevant to your employees. You should also consider whether your involvement of employees is sufficient. Involvement creates inspiration.

Examples of Lean

9

Lean has made noticeable improvements in agriculture and the food industry in recent years. The Lean thinking of reducing waste, creating structure and involving employees in continuous improvements fits perfectly with the many different jobs on a farm.

9.1 RESULTS WITH LEAN

9.1.1 THE PRODUCTION STRATEGY IS LEAN

Davidsen Landbrug A/S produces milk, and they have concentrated their production so that they focus on their core business – milk. They do not produce their young animals themselves, and they have outsourced their feed production. Kent Davidsen, who is one of the owners, says that it provides a structured day of work where it is possible to plan tasks and stay focused. They keep a very sharp eye on production costs, and with the specialized production, they avoid investing in something outside their core business.

When we ask Kent why they started working with Lean, he answers that to him it is a natural way to work. "Is there an alternative?" is his counter-question. He says that when he was alone on the farm, he could be everywhere. However, following the growth they have gone through, it is necessary to structure both work planning, performance management and continuous improvements. Lean thinking is perfect for this.

Kent further explains that they cut to the bone on costs and keep the focus tight. They continue along the path and are currently renting out all fieldwork. In return, they will invest in an extension for more cows.

> Lean thinking is necessary when you grow as we do. There are no alternatives.
>
> **Kent Davidsen**

One very central part of Lean thinking is that you focus on your main production as opposed to producing everything your assets, building, land, and machines tell you to produce. In Lean thinking, you concentrate your resources on optimizing the value for your customer.

9.1.1.1 THERE IS CONSISTENCY IN THE GOALS

For the company there are overall goals that are broken down into goals in four main areas and, in turn, broken down into day-to-days goals that can be acted on in daily operations. They currently have two farms, and there is a manager at each farm. The two managers conduct weekly board meetings with their employees where they are planning, performance managing and handling continuous improvements in production.

9.1.1.2 QUALITY IN THE WORK HAS IMPROVED

Manager Anders Jokumsen says that the Lean tools have given both him and the employees a better overview of production. They advance on the production results due to the systematics of the weekly performance management and of creating improvements.

Because the employees have been involved, the quality of work has improved. They can see how it affects the result when they do the work well, and they understand the background better. They have also become better at making decisions in their daily work. It saves the manager much time.

9.1.1.3 INVOLVEMENT CREATES COMMITMENT

At Davidsen Landbrug A/S, visible performance management is one of the much-used tools. The employees are involved in finding solutions, and they closely follow the results of their improvements.

Each time they reach one of their goals, it will be celebrated with cake. One of the employees even posted it on their Facebook page. It shows a true commitment.

9.1.2 IMPRESSIVE DECREASE IN COSTS AT ESBJERG DAIRY

Esbjerg Dairy has worked with Lean since 2007. Head of the dairy Jan Vrå Mikkelsen says that although there has always been work on optimizing the processes, there are some basic principles in Lean that have enhanced the dairy a lot.

JAN VRÅ MIKKELSEN

Head of Esbjerg Dairy Center since 2008. Esbjerg Dairy Center is an Arla Food dairy.
Experience with production management:
- Brewing master at Carlsberg
- Operational engineer at SAMDEN powder factory in Aabenraa
- Production Manager at Esbjerg Dairy

When asked what the effect has been, Jan Vrå Mikkelsen mentions conversion costs as an example. It is the cost of wages, energy, machinery, administration and so on – all the costs of converting the raw milk into the finished products. Conversion costs decreased 10% to 15% in the first three years with

Lean in spite of the fact that the general increase in wages, energy and so on in the same period was around 10%.

ESBJERG DAIRY

UHT (Ultra-high temperature processing) dairy with 250 employees
- Processes 175 million kg of milk per year
- Produces 485 different products, for example cocoa milk, sauces, soft ice cream, cream in Tetra Brik and so on.
- Esbjerg Dairy is one of the five most advanced UHT dairies in the world

---

9.1.2.1 BOARD MEETINGS ARE CRUCIAL

At Esbjerg Dairy, they used three to four of the Lean tools, but the board meetings were the foundation. They help motivate and maintain energy. "People have an influence on their everyday lives and their work. The board meetings are decision-making meetings, so if the employees want influence, they just have to show up", says Jan Vrå Mikkelsen.

He continues: "It is a different way to lead. We used to go and talk to a senior employee who got things working. Now we make things work at the board meetings, and those who have good input make the others join.

We have nine Lean groups who each have a board meeting of 15 minutes once a week. The improvement suggestions are prioritized and written on lists. During the week, they are carried out. That way, suggestions quickly turn into action".

9.1.2.2 5S PROVIDES SATISFACTION

"5S is undoubtedly the tool that most employees appreciate", says Jan Vrå Mikkelsen. "Creating and keeping order and systematics – putting common sense into system. Anyone can relate to and see the idea in that.

We have asked the employees if they are satisfied. They say different things, but everyone agrees that 5S has been good. The truth is that order makes happy, even with the most untidy persons. It is also a democratic process in which employees influence how things look".

9.1.2.3 START WITH ANALYSIS

Jan Vrå Mikkelsen says about the process, "We held workshops of two days for each production line, where we conducted value stream mapping. That is, we described the whole process and found out where it could go wrong. All sensors, lines, lanes and people – everything. Bottlenecks, waste, trouble. It may sound simple, but once you start working with it, you find out that there are actually more than 200 places where it can go wrong.

We grouped the 200 places into whether the problem was management, employees, planning, machinery, materials, etc. We prioritized them and suggested what to do better. The suggestions were written on sticky notes and discussed at board meetings. Since it is easier to get ideas than to implement them, some of the lines have made rules allowing only five ideas per week. All lines have made their own rules for the meetings and an operator – never a manager – is in charge of the meetings. That is important to us".

The results from the 16 lines in the period just after Esbjerg Dairy initiated the Lean process are shown in the curve below. "Efficiency has been improved by 10%, which means we can do more with the same people and the same capacity", says Jan Vrå Mikkelsen.

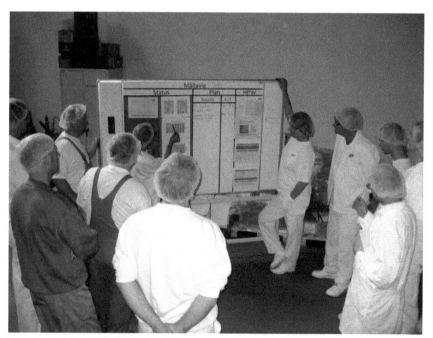

Board meeting at Esbjerg Dairy.

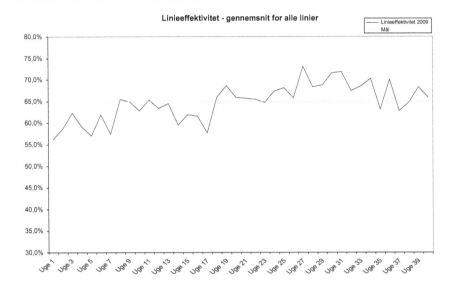

Result of the introduction of LEAN at Esbjerg Dairy
– Line efficiency increased by 10% the first year with Lean

9.1.3 LEAN – JUST COMMON SENSE

Johan Thuresson is an energy engineer, who after some years in Stockholm changed to farming. Today he runs a successful farm with hybrid gilt production in Sweden.

To the question why Johan chose to introduce Lean, he replied, "I have an engineering background and have previously been in contact with Lean thinking. Therefore, it was not hard for me to understand that Lean can also provide positive effects in agriculture. The idea was, and still is, to invest in what adds value and to reduce waste".

9.1.3.1 SPECIFIC EFFECTS

Lean has had several specific effects at the farm. "We have obtained a good structure in the short term through our weekly meetings and a good structure in the longer term through better planning, follow-up on performance and goals". Johan adds that he will also mention the importance of focusing on the value chain, standardization of routines, systematization and visualization, and it has become easier to handle deviations. "We have had a huge increase in production over the past year, and Lean has been an important piece in the puzzle".

> The idea was, and still is, to invest in what adds value and to reduce waste.

9.1.3.2 LEAN IS BASED ON THE COMMITMENT OF EVERYONE

When asked which challenges they have encountered, Johan answers: "We have had some staff turnover, and it is always a challenge to welcome a new person in the team. Lean is based on the commitment and Lean mindset of everyone, leader as well as employee.

Lean has provided us with tips on good tools to introduce new staff in a good way, and it usually works well. Basically, Lean is based on common sense, even if it is packaged in another form".

Management is important when it comes to Lean. Johan says management is something he constantly strives to develop, but it is also worthwhile, he says. It is often a big step to hand over control of certain points to your employees, but it is even better to see how the employees grow with their tasks.

Source: Johanna Andersson, Lean Landbruk, 2017.

Dictionary

10

We have chosen to explain some of the slightly special words we have used. It is not a complete list of Lean expressions.

10.1 DICTIONARY

5 x Why: A simple and efficient way to find the root cause of a problem: Ask "Why" and repeat the question five times.

Benchmarking: Comparing results and KPIs with other companies in the same profession. The purpose is to learn from the best.

Board Meeting: A brief standing meeting where employees are working with visible goal management and continuous improvements.

The Burning Platform: The (main) problem challenging the farm.

Coaching: A method that through questions and conversation allows the person him/herself to make suggestions for changes, activities and so on. The purpose is to develop and release the potential of the person.

Comfort Zone: The safe base you are in when there are no changes.

Continuous Improvement: This word covers the fifth Lean principle. It is about continuously improving workflows – it is about making it "a little better every day". It should be a culture at the workplace, so all employees are working on continuous improvements.

The Customer: The customer in the Lean context is the person/company receiving a benefit. It is not always an external customer, but can also be an internal customer, for example a colleague who is to continue the work on which another colleague has started. The internal customer can also be seen as the next link in the production chain.

Daniel T. Jones: Professor at Lean Enterprise Academy in England. With James T. Womack and others, co-author of many popular management books on Lean. He has contributed to spreading the knowledge of Lean all over the world. He is senior consultant at the Lean Enterprise Institute, management developer and mentor in the use of Lean in all types of companies. His speeches and lectures can be followed on YouTube and other sites.

Eiji Toyoda: Nephew of Sakichi Toyoda and head of Toyota Motor Company from 1950. Initiated the major restructuring of the company and the appointment of Taiichi Ohno, who developed the Toyota Production System.

Flow: Means that a task or item flows through the value stream without unnecessary stops caused, for instance, by defects or lack of information.

Gemba: Is Japanese and means production or where things happen. To go Gemba is about observing the value-creating activities with the purpose of understanding the processes and identify waste.

Goal Management: Goal management means that you actively and continuously monitor the performance of the processes in relation to the goal.

Hoshin Kanri: Is a method of breaking down the overall strategy for employee goals and actions. The purpose is to create coherence so that everyone at all levels of the organization works toward the same goal.

Internal Supplier: Supplier to deliver products within the farm. It may, for example, be the previous process in the production chain. The heifer barn is internal supplier of heifers for milk production, and the insemination unit is supplier of in-pig sows for the farrowing unit.

James T. Womack: Management expert and Ph.D. Together with Daniel T. Jones and others, he has written a number of books about Lean. He was the leader of the research team that introduced the concept of Lean Production after years of study of the Toyota Production System in Japan. He is co-founder of the Lean Enterprise Institute, a non-profit organization for the spread of Lean. He is now senior consultant at the Lean Enterprise Institute, and his lectures can be followed on YouTube and other sites.

Just-In-Time (JIT): Means a production system that produces and delivers exactly what is necessary – at the right time, in the right quantity and of the right quality, according to customer demand.

Kaizen: Kaizen is Japanese and means to change for the better. We call it continuous improvement. The manager must, deliberately and in a structured manner, motivate all employees to identify waste and make improvements.

Kanban: A signal from the subsequent process in the flow of a need for products or materials. Kanban may be on a card or other type of signal.

Kiichiro Toyoda: The son of the founder of Toyota, Sakichi Toyoda. In 1937, started the Toyota Motor Company.

KPI: Key performance indicator.

Lean: Means "trimmed". It is a method/philosophy that involves employees in optimizing value for the customer. It is done by continuously and systematically removing waste as well as getting processes and materials to flow without stop (create flow). It was the two researchers James T. Womack and Daniel T. Jones who "invented" the name.

Learning Styles: Means that we have different ways of learning.

Muda: Muda means waste in Japanese. Muda is central to Lean, and the word is used for what does not give value. Muda is one of the Three Wastes: Muda–Muri–Mura. Muri is unreasonable burden on people or machines. Mura is unleveled workloads on people or machines.

OEE: The capacity of a machine. The abbreviation OEE means Overall Equipment Effectiveness. It is one of the major measuring points in TPM (Total Productive Maintenance).

PDCA: The Plan–Do–Check–Act circle is a four-step model to systematically ensure that an improvement suggestion is planned, initiated, tested and implemented. The method can be used repeatedly with small improvements, so that you can experiment until the right solution is achieved.

Sakichi Toyoda: The founder of the Toyota family company. He changed the name because Toyoda means "fat rice field", which he did not think fit for a modern business.

SMART: Established goals must be SMART. That means that the goals must be: Specific, Measurable, Accepted, Realistic, Time-based.

SMED: SMED is short for Single-Minute Exchange of Die. It is a method to reduce changeover time on a machine.

SOP: Standard operating procedure: Description of a standardized work process. An SOP describes how a task should be done.

Standards: Standardized work is workflows that are determined to be the chosen best way to perform a process. It is very important that the standardized way is met, and corrections are made through continuous improvement work.

Taiichi Ohno: Was the factory manager and later became vice president at Toyota. He developed the concept of Just-In-Time and started the Toyota Production System.

Talking Stick: Based on ancient traditions, and over time has been used by many indigenous people when councils were held. It allows all members of the council to express their personal opinions, by passing the Talking Stick from hand to hand. Only the one who holds it is entitled to speak, and the others must listen.

TPM: Total Productive Maintenance. A systematic model for analyzing and improving a machine or other equipment's capacity utilization and involving employees who use the machine for continuous improvement and preventive maintenance.

TPS: Toyota Production System is a complete description of the tools developed by Toyota, which forms the basis of what we call Lean today in the Western countries.

Turn-around: Means turning a deficit business into a profitable business.

Value for the Customer: Customer value is an expression of what the customer will pay for and which has value to the customer. You should not produce anything that does not give value to the customer

Value Stream: Is a row of process steps needed to produce a product or a performance.

Value Stream Mapping: A standardized method of mapping how a product or service flows through the value chain. The purpose is to get a common picture of the situation and to identify waste, and then find improvement suggestions to remove waste.

Visible Goal Management: That everyone can see and keep track of how their efforts affect the results in relation to the goal.

Vision, Goal and Strategy: The vision is the company's overall idea of which direction it should develop. The goal is the vision expressed in benchmarks, so you can measure that you are on the way to the vision. The strategy is the method of reaching the benchmarks.

Waste: Waste is everything in the value stream that does not add value. There are eight wastes:

1. Defects
2. Overproduction
3. Waiting
4. Non-utilization of talent
5. Transport
6. Inventory
7. Motion
8. Extra processing

References

Andersen, Anders Bidsted and Henrik Tufvesson: *Lean-it- brug Lean, hvor det giver mening*, Børsens Forum S/A, 2006

Andersson, Johanna: *Bara vanligt bondförnuft på Löderups Gris*, Lean Lantbruk, 2017

Bak, Henrik: Global Lean Management, Arla (Personal Communication, 2011)

Balmer Hansene, Christian, Jens Stochholm Normand and Mikkel Simonsen: *Den gode leanleder*, L&R Business, 2010

Bicheno, John: *The Lean Games and Simulations Book*, Picsie Books, 2015

Bienhaus, Axel: Presswerk AUDI AG, www.forcam.de, 2017

Borup, Marianne: *Læringsstile*, www.mangeintelligenser.com, 2017

Bundgaard, Niels H.: *TPM, De Store tabsfaktorer*, Industriens forlag, 1999

Bundgaard, Niels H.: *TPM, Operatørstyret vedligehold*, Industriens forlag, 1999

Christiansen, Thomas B., Niels Ahrengot and Michael Leck: *Lean implementering i Danske virksomheder*, Børsens Forlag, 2006

Covey, Stephen R.: *The 7 Habits of Highly Effective People*, Simon & Schuster, 2013

Cullberg, Johan: *Kris och utveckling*, Natur og kultur, 2006

Danielsen, Henrik: Patriotisk Selskab (Personal Communication, 2011)

Davidsen, Kent: Davidsen Landbrug A/S (Personal Communication, 2017)

Dennis, Pascal: *Getting the Right Things Done*, Lean Enterprise Institute, 2010

Eriksen, Mikkel, Thomas Fischer and Lasse Mønsted: *God lean ledelse i administration og service*, Børsens forlag, 2005

Fenn, Jackie: *When to Leap on the Hype Cycle*, Gartner Group, 2009

Folkman, Bo: *Selvtilfredshed og den brændende platform*, www.Net-2change.dk, 2008

Ford, Henry with Samuel Crowther: *My Life and Work*, 1922

Grønkjær, Preben: *Forståelse fremmer samtalen*, Gyldendal Fakta, 2004

Hansen, Christian Balmer: m.fl.: *Den gode leanleder*, L&R Business, 2009

Jokumsen, Anders: Davidsen Landbrug A/S (Personal Communication, 2017)

Kotter, John P.: *Leading Change*, Harvard Business Press, 1996

Kotter, John P.: *Accelerate: Building Strategic Agility for a Faster-Moving World*, Harvard Business Review Press, 2014

Lean Enterprise Institute: www.lean.org, 2018

Lean Enterprise Institute: Lean Daily Forum, www.lean.org, 2018

Lean Lantbruk: *Bara vanligt bondförnuft på Löderups gris*, 2017

Lüscher, Lotte, Thomas Asmussen and Bent Vestergård: *Ledelse i Landbruget*, Landbrugsforlaget, 2014

Marchwinski and Others: *A Graphical Glossary for Lean Thinkers*, Lean Enterprise Institute, 2014

Martin, John: *Leadership for Dummies*, John Wiley & Sons, 2011

Millard, Maggie: www.KaiNexus.com, 2015

Medina, John: *Brain Rules*, Carlton North, 2014

Melander, Preben: *Lean med lederskab*, Jurist og Økonomforbundets Forlag, 2009

Mikkelsen, Jan Vrå: Esbjerg Dairy (Personal Communication, 2017)

Pejstrup, Susanne: www.LeanFarming.eu, 2018

Personalestyrelsen: *Anerkendende ledelse i staten*, www.perst.dk, 2008

Reid, Loy M.: *Learning Styles in the Classroom*, Heinle & Heinle Pupl., 1987

Richter, Mette: *Anerkendende ledelse – den nye ledelsesstil*, www.Mannaz.com, 2011

Rother, Mike and John Shook: *Lær at se, Kortlæg dine værdistrømme for at skabe værdi og fjerne spild*, Dansk Industri, 2003

Sayer, Natalie J. and Bruce Williams: *Lean for Dummies*, Wiley Publishing, 2007

Shook, John: *Managing to Learn*, Lean Enterprise Institute, 2008

Svendsen, Ann Møller and Jesper R. Hansen: *Målstyring – Enkelt og effektivt*, 2009

Svendsen, Ann Møller: Lean Akademiet (Personal Communication, 2017)

Sørensen, Mogens Egegård, *Lean Mindset and Coaching* (Personal Communication, 2017)

Tapping, Don and Tom Shuker: *Lean i service og administration*, Dansk Industri, 2005

Tennant, Charles and Paul Roberts: Hoshin Kanri: *Implementing the Catchball Process*, lrjounal.com, 2001.

Torreck, Pia: *Håndbog for nye ledere – Forretningsudvikling og personaleledelse i knæhøjde*, UPTION, 2009

Vaag, Michael: *TPM – Stabilitetsfundamentet for Lean*, Børsen Forum, 2006

Vaag, Michael: Valcon A/S (Personal Communication, 2011)

Whitmore, John: *Coaching på jobbet*, Peter Asschenfeldt nye forlag, 1998

Wilbek, Ulrik: *Tro på dig selv. Min vej til at udvikle og motivere mennesker*, People's Press, 2006

Womack, James P. and Daniel T. Jones: *Lean Thinking*, Simon and Schuster UK, 2003

Womack, James P.: *From Modern Management to Lean Management*, Lean Network Annual Conference, 2009

Index

Taylor & Francis Group
an **informa** business

Taylor & Francis eBooks

www.taylorfrancis.com

A single destination for eBooks from Taylor & Francis
with increased functionality and an improved user
experience to meet the needs of our customers.

90,000+ eBooks of award-winning academic content in
Humanities, Social Science, Science, Technology, Engineering,
and Medical written by a global network of editors and authors.

TAYLOR & FRANCIS EBOOKS OFFERS:

A streamlined
experience for
our library
customers

A single point
of discovery
for all of our
eBook content

Improved
search and
discovery of
content at both
book and
chapter level

REQUEST A FREE TRIAL
support@taylorfrancis.com

Routledge
Taylor & Francis Group

CRC Press
Taylor & Francis Group

For Product Safety Concerns and Information please contact our EU
representative GPSR@taylorandfrancis.com
Taylor & Francis Verlag GmbH, Kaufingerstraße 24, 80331 München, Germany

www.ingramcontent.com/pod-product-compliance
Ingram Content Group UK Ltd.
Pitfield, Milton Keynes, MK11 3LW, UK
UKHW021110180425
457613UK00001B/11